AF614391

FIVE YEARS IN REVOLUTIONARY CUBA

A MEMOIR

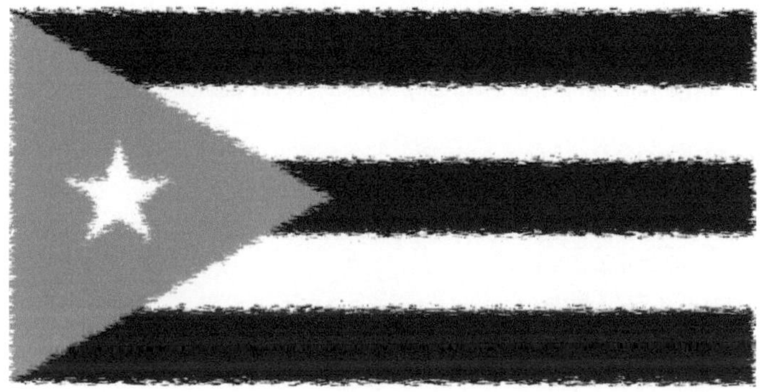

Carroll English

AuthorHouse™
1663 Liberty Drive
Bloomington, IN 47403
www.authorhouse.com
Phone: 1-800-839-8640

First published by AuthorHouse 10/8/2010

ISBN: 978-1-4490-7166-0 (e)
ISBN: 978-1-4490-7164-6 (sc)
ISBN: 978-1-4490-7165-3 (hc)

Library of Congress Control Number: 2010907822

Printed in the United States of America

This book is printed on acid-free paper.

Author's notes:

The names occurring in this book are the true names of the persons involved. However, since many of them have died, and I am no longer in touch with the rest of them, I am trusting that any persons still living who see themselves named here will not object to their inclusion in this account. Nothing scandalous or harmful has been said of them, and I wish them very well in their lives, wherever they may be.

The author is willing for portions of the text of this book to be copied and used by readers, as long as they ascribe proper credit and do not profit at her expense.

The Cuban spelling for the capital city of the island is *Habana*. The English spelling is *Havana*. Since I learned to use the Cuban spelling while being a part of that culture, I have used it throughout this book, to honor Cuba, Cubans, and the unique and delightful way of life that had been evolved there.

Carroll English
(carroll@stelle.net)

DEDICATION

The height of the Cuban revolution occurred during the three years that I lived in Habana, teaching at a Methodist girls' school. But my first two years in this small island nation were spent in service at an agricultural school at the far eastern end of the country. These years were filled with the excitement of living abroad for the first time, in total immersion in a new culture and a language I was still learning to express myself in, surrounded by fun-loving indigenous young people and conscientious, caring fellow teachers. At this institution, established on the worn-out soils where cane had been grown and harvested for many years, the students and faculty lived and worked together full time. Graduation would separate some of us each June. But this intensity of living together in an intimate and spiritually oriented intentional community knit us very close together.

We grew our own food, made it into very nourishing fare, ate beside each other at table three times a day, and I used a room in the girls' dormitory, since I was a young single missionary just out of college, and the dorm was the logical space available for me to reside in.

Even though over 50 years have passed, we have kept in touch with each other—faculty and students—uniting in reunions in Miami a number of times through the decades, and still communicating by mail, E-mail, and phone calls.

Truly, this sort of community seems like the ideal to me! I have always perceived what we had at "la granja" *as the best level of human social development. I agree with Mohandas Gandhi that the small village, where its members all know each other face-to-face and serve each other according to their talents and desires, is the very best form of human organization available. It is an extended family of primary relationships.*

Thus, even though it figures into this book very little, I dedicate this memoir to La Escuela Agrícola e Industrial Evangélica of Preston and Mayarí, Oriente, Cuba.

My memories of those two years remain vivid. Curiously, I am not currently in touch with any of my colleagues whom I knew in Habana, but I enjoy deep relationships with those I lived and worked with at the ag school.

Life at the ag school impacted my life in other ways, too. In 1967, I joined a philosophical community whose aim was to pioneer a finer society based on lifelong education and the pursuit of virtue. Though the character of this community of Stelle, Illinois, has changed about every decade, due to the accidents of history, I am still here over 35 years later, enjoying, as I may, the small-village life which we have here—though I am also willing for the community to grow into the great city we originally accrued here to build to support the establishment of the Nation/Kingdom of God on Earth.

CONTENTS

HOW I CAME TO GO TO CUBA

In college I changed my major several times—from agriculture (because I came from a family of farmers) to home economics (because I enjoyed the homemaking arts) to education (since all the women on both sides of my family had been teachers). I ended up with a BS in education from Florida State University, with a minor in Spanish. During my last year of college, reality was bearing down on me, of course. I knew that the protected life of student would soon be over, and upon graduation, I would be needing employment.

At that point in 1959, I didn't feel ready to settle down to teach who-knew-what in some little weed-overgrown town in south Florida where we were third-generation Floridians, as my father was hoping I would do. At this juncture in life, I wanted to see the world while I could. (My father himself had lied about his age during the First World War and joined the navy at 16, becoming acquainted with the European part of the world. During WW II he served in the Seabees in the South Pacific, experiencing the other half of the globe under Uncle Sam's auspices. Thus, my interest in seeing the world came from having heard Pa tell his adventure stories all my life!) And it seemed like the best way for me to see the world was to continue to expand my horizons from within my religious framework, the Methodist Church, which had at the time a variety of outreach programs. I hoped to be able to make a social contribution and experience distant cultures at the same time.

From childhood I had been a happily faithful attender of church and Sunday school. As a teenager I had continued active in youth folk-dance and discussion groups, then very popular in my denomination. Through the programs extant at the time within my church, I had in college traveled to New York City to visit the United Nations, to Washington to visit our representatives in the federal government, and to the Texas-Mexican border to participate in a church-sponsored work camp. In the work camp, we assisted to build, repair, and paint parsonages and churches of the Spanish-speaking congregations in the lower Rio Grande Valley, also teaching vacation-Bible-school classes to the Tex-Mex children in those little chapels.

Since I had avidly pursued Spanish in high school, I could somewhat defend myself in the language, and often served as translator for the work-camp group as we interfaced with the Spanish-speaking population among whom we worked. When we made a little foray into Mexico on a week-end lark once, I was almost detained at the border on suspicion that I was a Mexican trying to enter the U.S. with the returning group of Americans. While this occasion was a bit scary for me, it also made me happy at my achievement of a passable accent in Spanish after just a couple of years of the language in high school and a year in college.

My interest and proficiency in Spanish derived from the fact that I had been fascinated as a tiny child by the Cuban radio stations we could get in south Florida where I was born and reared. In those days there were no Mexican farm workers everywhere, as there are today in that state, and my family was mystified by my interest in what was a totally dead language to them. Even though there was no opportunity to study it until my junior year of high school, I grabbed onto it then with maximal interest, continually mumbling my vocabulary lists and verb conjugations to myself between classes and en route to school or home. I thus "tested out" of the first couple of levels of Spanish in college, based on what I had picked up in high school. This allowed me to go right into the 300 level at Florida State University.

By this time, I had seen too big a picture of the world as I was graduating from college to be willing now to just "settle down" in some little "Podunk" town and marry some guy who had never been anywhere or done anything out of the routine, and to live a conventional life. (Not that there is anything wrong with any of those things, I now very well recognize! There are times now when I feel that I missed a lot of what life normally is about by not living a more conventional life.)

Fortunately for me at the time, my natal church offered the means out of this dilemma of what to do with myself as I finished college. It gave members, especially young people, a chance to labor on the mission field for a period of three years without further obligation, in order to examine missions as a possible life vocation. Thus, I signed up for a stint at this, eagerly looking forward to where on the whole wide earth I might be sent for the next chapter in my life.

By that summer of 1954, I had been assigned by the Methodist Mission Board to Cuba as a short-term missionary. I was among the "LA-3's," or those going to Latin America for three years. Though it was designated as a three-year term, I stayed for five years, due to personnel turnovers of fellow missionaries in the field. (1954-9) And looking back, I can express considerable gratitude to the church and whatever destiny or karma placed me in that place at that time for that opportunity, as my life forever since has been greatly enriched by the experience!

This placement at that moment in history put me in an island nation which was ripe for revolution, due to the tenure in office of its iron-handed tyrant at the time, Fulgencio Batista—who was supported and sustained by the United States government in order to protect U.S. interests there—e.g., sugar, iron, and nickel companies owned by Americans, but above all, to maintain our military base on Guantánamo Bay. The base maintained our military presence in the Caribbean in the expectation that Communism would not dare to enter this theatre so close to the mainland of the United States of America. However, it was an illusion that it protected us in any substantial way from Communism, as later we were to discover that it was the very Achilles' heel, so to speak, through which Communism made its primary incursion into the Western Hemisphere through Castro's revolution.

Prior to traveling to my assigned field, I was among a group of varied Protestant neophyte missionaries who received preliminary training in Meadville, Pennsylvania. My fellows and the training faculty alike joshed me throughout the course for being sent to one of the major vacation playgrounds of the Western world—where, the implication was, I could hardly be expected to do any serious service. Being young and naive, I was caused to wonder whether I would indeed be doing any real work, given their jibes. Did they know something I didn't? I was not a playgirl type.

In any case, 1954 to 1959 when I was there, included the time building up to the Cuban revolution, the two years of the revolution itself, and some six months after Fidel Castro and the revolution came to power. I taught at the Escuela Agrícola e Industrial Evangélica near Mayarí and Preston at the far-eastern end of the island for the first two years, and then was sent to Colegio Buenavista, a school for girls in Marianao, a suburb of Habana, for the latter three years.

Our agricultural students in Oriente province were from deep in rural fields and mountains, with a portion of them being from the small towns of that province and its neighboring ones.

Ag student Emilio González works with the children of the cane cutters of a batey *on Sunday afternoons.*

At the ag school I taught English and a general orientation course called Understanding Myself that included fundamental housekeeping skills which all students were expected to learn, along with some crafts skills, some basic good manners, etc. I also played the piano at morning devotions, and did the payroll (of Cuban workers, such as the indigenous man who plowed with oxen for us, the Jamaican who ran our dairy operation, etc.) I lived in one of the girls' dormitories, which was like living with a number of sisters, as the female students were close to my age and were very warm and friendly—so typical of the Cuban character of that day.

Miriam and Caridad on the front veranda of Colegio Buenavista, the Methodist girls' school near Habana where author Carroll English taught for three years.

Ninth and tenth-grade Buenavista students in summer uniform.

In my final three years at Colegio Buenavista in Habana province, I taught fifth grade in English and some sixth-grade subjects, such as music and science. There was often a choir for me to direct, and the intramural sports program fell to me to conduct. Our team rarely won in its skirmishes with other girls' schools of the city, as I didn't really have any training for this and am not a fiercely competitive person myself. I've always believed that rabid competition causes more harm than good. My philosophy about sports has always been that if you're going to play, just play and have fun and do the best you can.

Colegio Buenavista kickball team. Author Carroll English in back, center.

This memoir is based on some passages that I sporadically recorded in a diary largely pertaining to the revolution, including also some excerpts from letters written home. The account is intermittent because I only wrote when salient events came to pass or when classes had to be suspended because of revolutionary activity in our area, making daily activity so dangerous that lives could not be risked to attend classes—at which times I had the leisure to write. I've also added some memories which came to mind in the process of inputting here the passages regarding political activity.

Of course every person's perspective is unique to him or her, according to background, training, life experiences, observation skills, etc. This is my account, and I will be as honest, sincere, and accurate as my faculties allow me to be.

Compare this building façade in Old Habana 50 years ago with the crumbling and unmaintained appearance of such buildings as seen on television today.

HOW I SAW THE CUBAN REVOLUTION: (TAKEN FROM MY DIARY)

The last election day under Batista's dictatorship:

November 3, 1958: Today was Tuesday, my birthday, (26 years of age)—a date around which elections are celebrated every two years in the United States. Likewise, Cuba's dictator Batista has selected the same first Tuesday in November for the national voting charade. This particular election has long been anticipated by everyone concerned with Cuba at home or abroad. People expect the worst, but with a (rumored) 20,000 militia to maintain the peace, the polls were opened. The great sorrow was—not the expected antics of rebels ripping up the country—but that a mere smattering of the population of voting age ventured to the polls. The streets of Habana and Marianao (where we live) were deathly quiet. The Chinese fruit vendor on the corner was the only person active in business in the whole neighborhood. All stores, banks, and schools were closed. Not even post-office employees worked today.

Miss Buck, the director of Colegio Buenavista, the girls' school where I live and work, heard several bombs go off last night and the night before. "Sources" claimed that some eleven bombs were exploded in the area, but we have no reliable information on this. We heard a shot tonight in our neighborhood. "Things" are happening, but we rarely get dependable knowledge of them through the rumor mill. These explosions and gun firings are sending a terrorist message to the population of Cuba:—probably something like: "Don't you dare go out there and participate in the political process! Drag your feet. Don't let the tyrant Batista think he is winning in any way!" Actually, it would not have mattered what the vote count was, as Batista would have won anyway, as dictators do. Thus, there was not much motivation to risk your life to go vote for a candidate you hated—or reveal yourself to the rebels who would not have appreciated your attitude of participatory citizenship.

President Fulgencio Batista Zaldívar, formerly a foot soldier in the Cuban military, had brought himself to power some years previously with a coup d' estat or a *golpe de estado* or a "blow to the state"—a military takeover. In these days of the new revolutionary menace, however, he is receiving the effects of the causes he put into action as a younger man, isn't he? "By what measure you give, so shall you receive."

Batista and his wife are very much reminiscent of Eva ("Evita") Perón and her Argentine-president husband, Juan Perón of the same era, in that they all consider themselves as benevolent parents to their respective nations of children. Both Eva Perón and her Cuban counterpart make big shows of their largesse at Christmastime by giving away massive quantities of gifts to poor children. While the two men make speeches about their fatherly generosity, their military fists of power are, behind the scenes, bashing anyone or anything that stands in the way of their getting what they want. Just the mere presence of a tyrannical rule such as Batista and Perón have established over their populaces is an immense insult to the people they govern and their intelligence! It is so galling! You continually feel treated like a child, and the expectation is that you will be compliantly obedient like a "good" son or daughter at all times!

We have heard that last Saturday night rebel hijackers forced a Cubana Airlines plane off its scheduled route from Miami to Varadero (Varadero is in the province adjacent to Habana at the western end of Cuba), demanding that it land at Preston (headquarters for the United Fruit and Sugar Company) at the far-eastern end of the island. The pilot obeyed the hijackers' demands but was unable to bring his plane down on the tiny runway there. He circled helplessly for an hour until ultimately the plane ran out of fuel and crashed into Nipe Bay below, killing all of those on board—all this taking place right out in front of the agricultural school there where I had worked my first two years in this country. Not many of the teachers and students remained at the school on account of the dangers of being anywhere but at home during times of political unrest. All of those left stood on the shore of the bay, watching helplessly throughout the entire process of the plane's destruction. Then it was they who had to dive beneath the murky waters to retrieve the bodies and artifacts. So sad and sobering for them!

Surely this tragedy could not help the rebel cause, I protest to myself! How can the rebels go on killing, destroying, forcing, terrorizing, etc., and still captivate the hopes, visions, and sympathies of the Cuban people! This is the expectation and nature of terrorism everywhere, though. And when enough people have been harmed or killed, ultimately the feelings of common folk become so aroused that they can be easily manipulated by a leader—and the desired chaos ensues. This is the stuff that war-makers use towards their ends!

The American Embassy in Habana is said to have sent investigators to the scene of the Oriente plane crash and expressed to the government on behalf of the United States an attitude of its being fed up with the kidnappings and confiscations by the rebels. These rebel capers were in the beginning seen as clever and amusing—but are very tiresome now. The Castro forces have grabbed jeeps, heavy equipment, men, and goods from the various American-owned mines and sugar companies in that vicinity. Some of the men I knew at Preston were taken as hostages by the rebels to be used to prevent the strafing of rebel mountain hideouts by government planes. Nothing seems sincere in such circumstances! All parties are using everything and everybody to force the accomplishment of their aims and desires!

All this activity is exciting to the common Cuban mind because of the anticipated freedom to be wrested from the dictatorship of Batista. The rebel leader, Fidel Castro, plays continuously upon pro-underdog sentiments, a vulnerable spot in the national thinking and feelings in a country where the vast majority of citizens are of the worker-farmer, lower-class segment of the population. Later we will go into detail about how Fidel systematically and constantly appealed to the Cuban mass of "little people" in order to build up a revolutionary force sufficient to taking over the country.

But if the U.S. government expresses anti-rebel sentiments too strongly, it seems entirely possible that Castro is liable to turn anti-American, which could affect the thousands of American citizens living and working here or visiting Cuban shores. Anti-American feelings have not been characteristic of Cubans in recent decades, but popular sentiment is with Castro now, so things could easily prove adverse for us residing here if he should get very upset with the United States at this point!

Dec. 2, 1958:

So many things are happening every day now, which should be recorded for history's sake. I must collect myself and start to commit to paper more events as I'm seeing them! I have hesitated to write down some of the horror tales of revolution which occur around us daily for fear that this diary might fall into the wrong hands and there be some kind of retaliatory danger to some of us, but truthfully, they should not be forgotten. They will be observations of a "mere bystander," as it has been pointed out to me—i.e., I "have lost no one in the conflict and will not lose anyone in it," as a fellow Christian and the minister of the church to which I belong throws up to me in our discussions of pacifism vs. war-making.

Scarcities suffered in the war zone:

Dr. Stewart, Cuban Methodism's lawyer and the district superintendent of this church in Oriente Province where the fighting is taking place, said three weeks ago that there was food for only 15 days more in that region. That time frame is now closed. Factories and businesses have shut down. It is said that farmers will not plant anything more, as (1) They are not able to sell products, the roads and other communications with the rest of the island being cut off, and (2) Crops have been burned and confiscated by government soldiers and by rebels, leaving the toiler no fruits of his efforts or investments. TIME magazine, our main source of news in Habana, has quoted some exaggerated prices which exist now as a result of the shortages. We wonder what people will do when the money and the residues of food stocks run out.

Electricity in Oriente has been cut off for weeks. It was said that water had become unavailable, but evidently it has been restored, as we've heard nothing more about that matter. For some two years now, the army of Batista has struggled fiercely with the opposing rebels in the provinces at that far end of Cuba (Oriente, Camagüey, and Las Villas). The rebels shoot up a town or bomb its facilities, government planes strafe the hillsides, and flamethrowers easily torch the thatched *bohíos* (country homes). I hate to think of the ruination of that beautiful land of which I became so fond when I first came to Cuba!

Capitol building and surrounding park in Habana. Capitol is obviously modeled after that of the United States.

U.S. government's involvement in Cuba:

Today the rumor was that Secretary of State John Foster Dulles has sent for Ambassador-to-Cuba Earl Smith to come to Washington for talks. Could this Republican administration be waking up to the fact that Cuban-U.S. policy needs to undergo some thoughtful changes? Latin Americans long for a Democratic administration in the American seat of government. They fondly remember F.D. Roosevelt and the "good days" under that party's charge. I heard someone exclaim today, "What can you expect when a militarist (Eisenhower) is President! And he is also a Republican as well!" (I.e., less inclined to offer aid to smaller nations.)

The United States still officially recognizes President Batista, sends him military strategists, has supplied him with arms—though they are slowing down on this now since the arms are causing so much havoc—and yet must make concessions to Batista's demands in order to maintain him as a "watch dog over our bulwark against Communism in the Caribbean," that is, so that he will protect our Guantánamo base in Oriente Province. The specter of Communism is used so affectingly by the Eisenhower administration to keep us locked into (what we later came to call) the "Cold War!" Could Communism be any worse than a regular old-time dictator who has now oppressed, killed, and maimed so many thousands here over the space of his tenure! More on this later.*

Maybe it seems so in Washington, which is at so safe a distance from here, but certainly not here in Cuba! I've never met any American who ever noticed that our dogged clinging to the Guantánamo base did not save us from Communism in the Caribbean!

Later, in 1960 and '61, when the United States rejected Castro's early gestures of friendship, Fidel was forced to appeal to the Soviet Union and China for aid. The Soviet Union's then-president, Nikita Khrushchev, saw its relationship with Cuba as an opportunity to sneak in some inter-continental missiles to hide in the Cuban mountains of the same province where

---

* Later it became known that, yes, a Communist Stalin could be worse than a small-time tyrant like Batista. Joseph Stalin was responsible for the deaths in his gulags of some 16 million persons, while Cuba's total population at the time was only six million! Compare these to China's Mao Ze Dong, who was responsible for the demise of 300 million!

the Guantánamo Base was located. When these were observed from the air by a U.S. spy-reconnaissance plane, the young President Kennedy stepped up to the plate and confronted the Soviet leader about them. Khrushchev was as afraid of nuclear war as Kennedy, so he had to back down and out of Cuba. We now know (but didn't at the time) that those missiles were quite primitive—not capable of going very far or with any accuracy at all. Even if we had realized that, the "Cuban missile crisis" might still have been unavoidable, as these propelled vehicles might still have been able to devastate some of the southern-American states. In contemporary times we have found out that Russia only had a total of four intercontinental missiles, while the U.S. had hundreds (per Richard Rhodes in ARSENALS OF FOLLY), so we need not have been so fearful in our response, but of course we were ignorant of it at the time.

Actually, it has also become understood in recent times (2008) that Fidel never really intended to establish a democratic government, as it had already been noticed by Che Guevara among the Cuban revolution's political elite that the United States destroys democratically elected governments and only deals with dictators. (If we just look around in history, we will see that this is absolutely true! If we mere citizens had understood this back in '59 and '60, we could have much earlier in the game saved ourselves a lot of conjecturing and wondering about what Castro was actually up to! If we had understood this connection, which jeopardizes new leaders in terms of their relations with the U.S., we would perceive more clearly what Venezuela's current president, Hugo Chavez, is up to and why he keeps his distance from the United States. His mentor and model is Fidel Castro, as is well-known.)

In any case, upon reaching the pinnacle of power in Cuba, Castro was looking for allies, as he had no capital with which to establish what he had in mind to do for Cuba. For this reason, he appealed to the largest world nations for aid (the U.S., the Soviet Union, and China).

Church minister imprisoned by Batista:

Dec. 14, 1958: At last we know where our preacher friend Mario Fernández is and that he is still alive. He is charged with being complicit with the rebel enemy of the regime and will be placed in the Príncipe Prison, a large old fortress used for the detention of political prisoners here in Habana, where he will be able to receive needed food and clothes through visits from those close to him. We pass the Príncipe every time we drive into the city of Habana. It is on the river which divides it from its adjacent city of Marianao where our girl's school is.

Miss Buck (my school's director), Dr. Carlos Pérez (director of Candler College, the boys' school across the street from us), and his wife Luisa, and Ildeliza, (Mario's wife), went this afternoon to take Mario some bed clothes. However, he was *incomunidado*, and they weren't permitted to see him.

It is said that he has not been mistreated—and it could be so, as the father of a close preacher friend of his is police sergeant in the same station where he has been held. This friend has spared nothing, not even risk to his reputation and that of his father, to try to find out where Mario was, learn what was happening to him, and figure out how to get him out of confinement, if possible.

But Dr. Pérez has also been working on the matter day and night, courageously pulling every string or *palanca* (lever) possible, trying to discover what is happening with him. Someone who was in a position to know warned him that if he was going to do anything about Mario, he had better do it quickly, implying that he is in imminent danger. Thus, everyone who has been involved in his case has fervently renewed their efforts.

Dr. Rodríguez, head of the Evangelical Seminary of Theology down-island in Matanzas, came with all haste to endeavor to work through an acquaintance of his named Ballart, who is said to be Batista's right-hand man.

Meanwhile, Ildeliza is the cousin of the wife of the head of SIM, Cuba's FBI, and has been frantically trying to move events through that contact. Mario has a cousin who is quite high up in the Cuban army. All Mario's family members and friends have been at telephones day and night in the service of this cause.

Mario's wife Ildeliza stayed here (at Colegio Buenavista) most of the day, crying or pensive, close to Miss Buck, who is ever-ready to console, especially in the case of Mario, whom she has always treated and loved as a son.

Fellow Habana ministers, Ernesto Vasseur and Jorge León, have also been on constant call and in vigilance on behalf of their friend Mario.

Our most pressing hope is that the government has not mutilated him! Someone was saying the other day that several persons they knew, including close relatives, had been forced to appear, smiling, in visits with their family members, as though they had been well-treated—while in reality, their bodies—except for visible hands and faces, were raw pulp from the beatings and tortures. Some people have had their eyes gouged out. One wife discovered, when she claimed the crumpled body of her husband who had been hanged, that he had been sat in a chair without a seat, under which a fire had been set. Another lady suffered severe internal hemorrhaging and injuries, wavering on the brink of death from the brutal torture by Batista's soldiers—until by some miracle she was able to be whisked from the country and taken to Venezuela. The same torturers burned the soles of a young man's feet in order to make an example out of him, in case anyone doubted the ruthlessness of the Batista regime. The boy was innocent of what he was accused of, but it was said that as he lay writhing in pain for days until his feet could heal, he plotted to wreak vengeance upon his captors.

And thus the stories go, on and on. We hope that none of these maimings have occurred to Mario! The more tense this conflict becomes, the more depraved the tortures become! Is there something in the male/macho mentality that believes that the more harmful the punishment, the greater deterrent it becomes? Research and practical observation show that nothing could be further from the truth! "More flies are caught by honey than vinegar" could be applied, rather than torture. There are ways to reward the desired behavior and downplay the undesired acts! "Confessions" wrung out of tortured prisoners are entirely unreliable, as history has shown over eons. We ourselves and almost everybody we know could easily reach a breaking point under sufficient duress and tell captors anything they wanted to hear! Surely the fact is that torturers become caught up in a certain pleasure derived from harming others, from wielding their little teaspoonful of power over others.

Likewise, capital punishment has been shown to essentially not relate to the behavior of people who kill others. Instead of punishing criminal behavior, a more effective system should be devised to cause the perpetrators to make complete restitution for damage done, in my view! A killer would have to support for the rest of their lives the family members left behind by the person he killed, etc., for example. Retaliation by the system upon those they suspect of having committed crimes continues the painful cyclical interaction, tit for tat forever, never truthfully serving justice—unless intelligent action be brought to bear to intervene. (But is that ever done?!)

The macho egomaniac seems to perpetrate upon the rest of us a certain tunnel vision on this score, in my perspective! I have become more persuaded of this, my position on torture, the longer the public has had to be subjected to the "controversy" played out in the press over the Iraq-war treatment of prisoners in our present time! Having taught in a prison here in Illinois, including ministering to the women on Death Row, I still feel strongly that our whole "justice system" creates an enormous amount of injustice and further crime! We cannot even rationally look at this matter long enough to create a better system, however, because of the greedy frenzy around the whole detention system—i.e., so many persons are making so much money off prisons and jails that we may be assured that nothing will be allowed to change! Well, this might be an apt subject for a different publishing event!

Returning to Rev. Fernández' imprisonment, Miss Buck said that Mario's interrogators had asked him, "Why does an honest, educated man such as you get mixed up in something like this (the revolution)?" But of course they know what everyone knows—that the educated and professional people are the ones who are the strongest opponents of a dictator and the first to enlist in an idealistic cause—which has been true in Russia, Germany, China, and all over the world!

Do ends justify the means?

Any lofty ideals which anyone on either side may have had in the beginning of this fracas have long since and many times over been compromised and tested when the pressure of reality has caused them to do things expediently and in desperation. In reality, nothing is fair in (love and) war, contrary to the popular adage. In war, certainly, people become motivated by hate, fear, pride, desperation, etc. If these work their way into the means of human conflict, how can any ends derived from them be acceptable! It certainly seems true that just any desired ends do not justify any unjust means, no matter how desirable they may appear to those who espouse them at some point in time!

Speaking in 2009, I can say that I have not heard debates on making peace for some years! When I was in high school and college, the themes of the justification for war and avoiding war were front and center in our youth groups and in the Wesley Foundation discussion groups. Pacifism was then a very viable philosophic position. I have a friend who was a conscientious objector during the Vietnamese War, but so many of our long-honed American values seem to have died during that conflict! Presently, a pacifist position is considered to be anti-patriotic! But let us continue with my thought process regarding revolutionary Cuba in 1958-9:

Surely it is true that "All who take up the sword will die by it"—at least for those who have agendas of greed, fear, or hate when they take it up. And he who helps to lift the arm that wields the sword in greed, fear, or hate is about as guilty as the hand which brandishes it, isn't he?

On the other hand, taking up arms in self-defense is surely justified. How to distinguish any reasonable taking up of the sword from unreasonable and unjust taking of it is where the matter all comes to lie. What is true about taking up weapons in this revolution, I wonder? Ethics should be easy, usually—you *do what is best for the greatest good of all concerned.* Do to others what you would like to have done to you. That is the big secret of ethics, isn't it?

We've gotta go to a movie!

I know that I would not like to be shot at or maimed for life by a terrorist shell or bomb. Yet on the other hand, it feels like we can't live in fear all the time, hiding out in the boarding department of our school week after week, month after month. Sometimes we two younger missionaries feel like we've just got to go to our little local neighborhood movie house and risk whatever there is to risk. The two older missionary ladies always try to dissuade us of such fool-heartiness with somber words about not wanting to be "blown up by a terrorist bomb or live in a handicapped condition for the rest of our lives." Fortunately, we're surviving so far, despite having taken in two or three films at the little out-of-the-way theater two blocks away from our school! (We seemed to be cases of youth characteristically believing that they will live forever!)

Missionary personnel at Colegio Buenavista, c. 1953: Miss Juanita Kelly, interim director; Barbara Smith Theis, fellow LA-3; Miss Valerie Grubb, retired volunteer; authoress Carroll English.

Oppression brings desperation:

Mario Fernández, our minister friend, was accused of selling *bonos* (tickets) to raise money for the revolutionary cause. Is this wise? I wonder. It seems to me that one who has a family and represents the church, as a minister does, must think of the possible effect on those around him if he is caught. Now Mario's family is broken and heart-broken, the church has jeopardized its position and name to try to save him. He is receiving who-knows-what-kind-of treatment. The effects of his actions are returning to haunt him. Now is not a time to say, "I told you so," however. We can see how desperate people become under oppression!

The revolution triumphs: January 1, 1959.

Now, nearing 11:30 P.M., on one of the most memorable days in Cuba's history, what one hears at this moment are the neighborhood radios. The station called *Radio Reloj* (Clock Radio) is blaring the latest news and messages from Fidel Castro. And police sirens are going off, and the occasional drone of an airplane landing or leaving the Colombia Air Field nearby (going to or coming from Miami to return the exiles to their homeland, people imagine).

We being cloistered away in our boarding-school home, the students having gone home for the holidays, this morning began for us missionary staff like every one this vacation: Breakfast at 7:30 in the now-empty sun-lit dining hall, the French doors opening onto the garden, bright with yellow cana lilies and flaming bougainvilleas, the gentle tinkle of the service bell calling the servant in to bring more bread or coffee. The morning devotional was read among us all, as always.

After the meal, we retired to sew upstairs. But soon Miss Buck came puffing into view at the head of the stairs, asking excitedly, "Have you heard the news?" She spilled out to us all that she had heard it rumored that dictator Batista had fled by plane this morning during the wee-small hours, absconding for parts as yet unknown.

About this time, we began to notice automobile horns blowing in the street outside, and voices shouting something. The Catholic-church bells in the vicinity were tolling on and on—and had been for some time, we realized. Neighborhood boys began popping the remnants of the fire crackers they had used last night to blast in the New Year.

Changing the dial from our music station to one of the news stations, we found that the entire program consisted of the latest dispatches—announcing that the dictator and forty of his henchmen had fled this morning by plane to Santo Domingo; a military junta is meeting to name a provisional president and to provide for free elections as soon as possible, etc. Then the National Anthem would play. Then, "Fidel Castro, from his position in the Sierra Maestra mountains, sends this message to the citizens of Cuba: 'Keep calm, and don't do anything which would cause more bloodshed. Fly the Flag of Freedom!' " (I.e., the Cuban national flag, as opposed to the rebel one which had been clandestinely circulating throughout the revolution), implying that Cuba is now freed by the revolution and can go back to using the regular symbol of free Cuba instituted after the Spanish-American War wrested the country from Spain's grip.

Mary Cabrera, fellow teacher, came charging up the stairs shouting, *"¡Viva Cuba libre!"* (Long live free Cuba!), giving us big hugs and launching into rapid-fire details of the dictator's alleged escape and what the ostensible plans were as they were developing from Fidel's Rebel Headquarters in the mountains.

According to her sources, President Batista had reportedly been confronted last night at a dinner with all his military heads, they expressing that they would no longer stand for more of his regime. He was said to have stuttered around, gathered up a few personal belongings, boarded a plane in the early hours of the morning, and hastily departed, though it was also rumored that all of the henchmen fled with him on the same flight.

By 4:30 A.M., Mrs. Sánchez (one of Colegio Buenavista's teachers) was calling other teachers to proclaim freedom in the land. At 5:00 A.M., William Smith, a close friend of Mary's, was banging at her front door, shouting that Cuba was free at last.

People of the public dragged out from hiding an array of rebel flags, large and small, and hung them out on their balcony or put them on the hoods of their cars, riding up and down the streets, blowing the horns and shouting, *"¡Viva Cuba libre!"* or put them on their person as they promenaded the streets.

The horizontal upper half the rebel flag is red and the lower half, black, with the number 26 in white in the very middle. The twenty-six refers to the 26th of July, 1953, when Fidel and way-breaking revolutionaries made their first move by attacking the Moncada fortress in Oriente province.

Now in the flush of revolutionary triumph, everyone who had red-and-black clothing put it on immediately and rushed out into the flood of rejoicers—this, despite Castro's warning to stay at home and not cause disturbance. The radio brought orders from the American Embassy, telling Americans in Cuba not to go out, not to participate at all in the commotion. (Two days ago, two Americans were pulled off a loading plane at Habana's Rancho Balleros Airport at gun point by plainclothesmen, because they had expressed some pro-rebel opinion during their stop-over there between Jamaica and the U. S. They had been taken to prison, and the Embassy was embarrassedly and nervously investigating the case.)

Fellow missionary Marshall Lindsay came walking in at lunch, having just arrived at that same airport. He told us that the celebrators were slap-happy in all parts of the city, running through red lights and committing every imaginable caper. People all over town were calling up and visiting friends to share their elation, now that the tensions of censorship, wire-tapping, and secret police had suddenly evaporated.

LA-3 missionary Marshall Lindsay teaching a class of boys of Candler College and girls from Colegio Buenavista, two Methodist schools across the street from each other.

An aftermath of lawlessness:

<u>But as the day wore on:</u>

⋆Some people have mistreated and killed some of the *"chivatos"* (spies, stool pigeons). In the town of Cruces, near the city of Cienfuegos, the people of the city recently rose up to slaughter all of these suspected *chivatos* among themselves, while the rebel radio ineffectually pleads for them to leave the execution of justice to the rebel chiefs. One *chivato* near us here was beaten, kicked, and mauled—probably killed. This is a sorry price to pay for the meager $33.33/month which spies on government payrolls received. Colleague Mary Cabrera states that the rebels have the lists of the *chivatos* in hand, so that everyone will soon know who was indeed a government spy. (In February of '59, the following was added as a marginal note in my diary: "It seems that lists were not available. Instead, the filled-out checks which were ready to be distributed to those who had provided the Batista government with covert information were somehow obtained. Also, anyone whom others had merely denounced as having been an informant were caught and harmed. It has become obvious that anyone who had a vendetta against another could simply point the finger of accusation at them, and their case would be "handled." Conceivably many injustices may be being perpetrated by the ease with which this naming of one's enemies can take place.)

⋆There have been many car accidents in these days of delirium—two or three at least in the immediate neighborhood. No one respects traffic signs or laws, now that "We are free!"

⋆By now, several records of the "National Anthem," the *"Himno Invasor,"* must have been worn out by Radio Progreso

Nacional as it played these over and over and over. Early this morning, radio announcers were giving their play-by-play accounts on the public air waves in their practiced unemotional voices—but by tonight, they were betraying many emotions as they spoke of the "new birth of democracy" or relayed the latest instructions from Rebel Headquarters in Oriente.

Street scene in Vedado, a Habana suburb, looking toward the city of Habana.

*Political prisoners must have been released because we were called and informed that the detained minister, Mario Fernández, was with his wife and two small children. (Later: the newspaper revealed that the "moles" (*chivatos*) had released the prisoners. They doubtlessly wanted to appear in the proper spirit of the new national life, perhaps in an effort to save themselves from mob violence for having been stool pigeons to the Batista government.

No longer do we have that heavy preoccupation hanging over us of "What will be the outcome of Mario's trial on January 12th?" or "Will he be released as we hope?" Now our questions tend along these lines: "Will he be able to go to the States to get him away from the heavy political milieu he got himself into?" "Will Ildeliza go with him, as she wants to do—or have to remain here with the children, cooped up with them and her mother in the one room they share at the Metodista Central church?" Etc.

A couple of days ago when we were still under the Batista regime, Jorge León, minister at the Metodista Central Church, was detained and questioned as he entered Príncipe Prison to visit Mario. He was warned not to come to see him anymore—or he would be "suspected"—meaning: caught, imprisoned, etc. So he had decided not to go back anymore—for the sake of all concerned. Fortunately, we don't have to worry about this threat at this point.

⋆The mobs, in their agitation, have broken and entered, pillaged and burned many establishments of persons they knew or suspected of being pro-Batista—while Castro calls from the hills to stop it. "We are still not free from the military junta! We must stick together and remain calm! We need the goods that are being destroyed in the rioting!" (And he was so right! Fifty years later, the scarcities in Cuba have never abated!)

⋆Drunken brawls have broken out wherever there is a corner bar. The "voice from the hills" commands that no more liquor be sold or consumed—but who is there to enforce these edicts?

Missionary buddy Marshall Lindsay and I went out into the neighborhood today to take pictures of the celebrating, stopping at the corner store for a cold drink. Men were milling around inside, as usual—but there were more of them on this occasion, all idle, drinking, talking. Before we could get our drinks, the owner began closing the doors, slamming them in anger, and verbally moving the customers out. These idlers had been drinking plenty and paying little, apparently. We realized that a ruckus was commencing inside the shop and that we were being locked inside with it! Drunken men don't like to be forced or tampered with. Together, Marshall and I were able to wrench the nearest door open and slip out as quickly as possible. There wasn't time to be afraid, but afterwards we realized that the situation had a considerable potential for trouble.

⋆The country is organized for a general strike, step-by-step orders coming from the crackling, variegated-wave-length rebel station from Santiago de Cuba. This is intended to force the military junta's hand. The latter proposes a man named Piedra as the provisional president, while Castro has named a man named Urrutia, former magistrate of Cuba who was exiled for his "administration of justice in the face of Batista's governmental oppression."

⋆The sugar harvest was to begin tomorrow. It will not, however. No one will move out of his home tomorrow, no one will work, save those employed by the press and radio stations, so as to keep confusion at a minimum, keep pressure against the military junta at a maximum, and keep the public informed and organized.

⋆Today, everyone is a rebel. People who were pro-Batista are gaudily displaying their supposed support of the rebels and the new freedom with their dress in the rebel colors, red and black.

In which political direction will the country go?

What does this day ultimately hold in meaning for Cuba and Latin America? Is this really the happiest day in Cuba since it gained its rudimentary democracy decades ago—or is it to be one of the saddest ones in Cuban history, in the final analysis? Will democracy be possible after this immense upset of the status quo? Will any kind of organization be possible after this chaos—or will it take another hand as iron-clad as Batista's to bring the situation under control?

I rather suspect the latter, as do most "thinking" persons I know. Or will there be another unsuspected result?

No one ever dared hope that Batista would leave the Cuban scene. Turns out he is presently residing with his old enemy-now-friend who just sent him 30 airplanes—Trujillo of the Dominican Republic. (Contemporary [2008] author, T.J. English, writer of HABANA NOCTURNE on the effects of organized crime under Batista's rule, has recently revealed that Batista had been being paid off so handsomely by the U.S. Mafia at this point in his regime, that he was safely spending most of his time living in Daytona Beach, Florida, far from the menace of the Castro revolution.) Batista-ites, his supportive partisans left back in Cuba in 1959, had looked forward to the day when Batista would put the rebel upstart Castro under his heel—while those of rebel sympathies had expected to see Castro walk into Habana any day now for at least two years.

We have heard by the grapevine that thousands have been killed in the cities of Santa Clara and Cienfuegos down the island during the last few days by bombings from "government planes." We don't yet know whether they are Trujillo's or the U.S.A.'s or some other country's—or the reason for the destruction. Important buildings there have been destroyed. We wonder about our church workers there. With such widespread damage and house-to-house fighting, they have been in extreme danger, for sure. We here in Habana truthfully know nothing of the rigors of open warfare as they have known it in the interior of the island. Fie on this fighting! One feels frustrated, angry, and inadequate to bringing about any useful change in this situation!

There must be some kind of discipline or the citizenry will destroy itself! Here in Marianao the police have been shooting on sight anyone whom they perceive as trouble-makers or anyone who might be in the wrong place at the time. Who knows, from a larger perspective, who is in the right and who is in the wrong? We haven't been able to discover details about any recent events. Since I have been writing here, I have heard a number of shots close by and the almost-continual whir of incoming and outgoing planes.

All flights scheduled for tomorrow have been cancelled, of course. Missionary friend Barbara Smith then cannot visit her brother in Miami, as planned. I pray for wisdom as to what we must do, how we should talk, what and how we must think in order to respond best in the present situation!

The radio is key to public control in the chaos:

January 5, 1959: The key to the organization of the rebellion has been the radio. On the 1st of January, all stations tuned into one wave link. A Panamanian station and one in Venezuela were included in the Rebel Network *("Cadena Rebelde").* Play-by-play descriptions of the events of the day in the different parts of the island were reviewed on air, and in Habana in particular, these were spoken in the rapid-fire staccato manner of the news stations here. Everyone remains glued to the radio to hear orders as they are handed down by rebel hierarchy.

The life histories of the man Urrutia, the rebel-named provisional president, and of "the glorious rebel leader of the 26th-of-July Movement, Dr. Fidel Castro Ruz," were repeated *ad infinitum* throughout the 3rd and 4th of January. On the lst and 2nd, the air waves carried mostly instructions for citizens, calls for Dr. So-and-So, and appeals for ambulances to rush to this or that address, calls for blood donations with the promise of free transportation, repeated commands to remain calm so as to avoid further bloodshed, repeated commands that only authorized cars were to be on the streets, calls for gasoline for Red Cross vehicles, ambulances, and military cars, calls for the youth militia to go quickly to such-and-such an address where a house was being ransacked, emergency calls for Commander So-and-So, for *"Fulano,"* (So-and-So) to call such-and-such a phone number, announcements of a students' meeting at the university at 10:00 A.M., announcements of a workers' meeting in Central Park (*Parque Martí*) to plan the strike (in order to force the military junta out of the picture and stall the rabble until order can be established), etc. They began interviewing rebel heroes on the radio and TV by the 3rd of January and filling in a great deal of air time with messages from rebel soldiers to their families at home.

This communications hook-up was an effective way to manage the scene, the whole island being tuned into the one station. This made the listener feel as though he were on the inside of the whole operation, hearing all the internal workings of organization in the dawning of the new year of national life. "New year, new life!" an old saying goes. And "A new broom sweeps clean!" were adages repeated often by many lips.

Cuba being so small (about the size of Florida) makes for a cozy feeling of family closeness and familiarity in this historic moment. Seems that all want to feel "on the inside," and push themselves into that circle as much as they can. The revolution has brought a greater sense of unity to national life—after the years of "we and they" during the struggle of rebels against the Batista regime. The majority of the population has been working all this time—hoping, planning, praying for the day that Castro's movement would triumph and Cuba would become a free, democratic land—the dream of Jose Martí, the national hero, the Father of his Country who cultivated this *sueño* (dream) among Cubans decades ago.

Grocery stores may open:

The strike, which was finally lifted last night, lasted long enough for many people to become very hungry. Yesterday morning the word came over Radio Rebelde that grocery-store owners could be added to the list of those who were authorized to work. Up to this point, those who were given permission to be gainfully employed during the strike were medical workers, those connected with the militia and radio, and airplane pilots bringing exiles from Honduras, Venezuela, Mexico, Guatemala, Colombia, and the United States. These selected employees seemed to revel in the importance that this honor gave them.

This new permission must have brought a feeling of relief to the *bodegueros* (grocery-store owners), as they had been having to sell food to the public clandestinely—making storeowners feel very nervous as they risked being caught and punished. The morning of the 4th, there were long lines of hungry citizenry at the back door of every grocery store, no matter how small or large the establishment may have been. As of today, grocery stores are allowed a two-hour opening each day until the strike's end.

Later, these shortened hours were still appropriate, because food supplies have been scant for the several intervening years since the revolution started in earnest. And it has continued for years afterward! Citizens have had to stand in line, sometimes for hours, and receive whatever foodstuffs were available—not whatever they had wanted to buy. And reportedly one would receive one's dole in a brown paper bag—to discover later that the meat portion they had brought home for the family to nurture itself on consisted of lumps of fat and a bone. (We in the U.S. heard early-on after the revolution took over that to be able to get an orange—in the land where Christopher Columbus brought and established citrus trees—one had to have a doctor's prescription, on account of the scarcity of citrus, due to the populace's hunger. And since stealing is so universally prevalent in Cuba today, the only piece of fruit one may be able to procure, even with a medical prescription, may be a runty little hard, green ball—at least until very recently when permaculture-teaching foreigners have taught the common citizens to grow their own food in vacant lots and fields—and even on balconies and rooftops. We haven't heard yet whether they are free of pillage, however.)

Abundant displays of tropical fruit could be seen throughout the city while there was political stability under Batista. However, there was a "special period" in Cuba after the revolution's triumph in which the populace was at the brink of starvation on account of the lack of capital, employment, internal production of food, etc. Fortunately, Permaculturists from outside the country rose to the occasion and promoted the cultivation of foodstuffs in vacant lots, fallow fields, rooftops, etc. Growers were allowed their profits, even under Communistic control, so that food is more abundant now and citizens are encouraged to produce food.

Popular combat songs:

Back to the news of the opening days of the new regime: Several combat songs have come out of the fracas. They are not particularly good, but having been recorded illegally in Mexico and sung among the rebel groups, they are fraught with meaning and glory now. These have been played over and over on the radio. One of them is prefaced by machine-gun fire, a plane roaring overhead, and exploding bombs, before the music finally commences. The piece ends in the same dramatic manner.

International response to the new Cuba:

The radio has announced the arrival of each plane as it has grounded, full of returning exiled youth—34 on this flight, 72 on that one, etc. The announcer also gives the names of those who have figured in well-known rebellious acts against the Batista regime.

Cuban students in Spain have wired their felicitations and assurances that they were giving ample thanks to the Virgin of Cobre, Cuba's patron saint, to whom they had prayed so fervently "for this great liberation."

Shrine of la Virgen del Cobre, Cuba's patron saint. She is said to have appeared to and saved three drowning men in a storm.

There had been a large picture of dictator Fulgencio Batista with the Flag of September 4th, his personal flag commemorating his assumption of power, displayed beside the Cuban flag over every police and rural-guard station, army post, and school in this country and the Cuban Embassies in other countries. The ones over the embassy in Mexico were said to have been taken out into the embassy gardens there today by exiled Cubans and burned with great fanfare.

We hear radio messages from exiles in many countries to the Cuban people in the new "land of the free," exclaiming their joy in their anticipated re-unification with their families in their native homeland during the days to come.

We go on an outing to survey the scene:

On the afternoon of January 3rd, Rev. Moreno and his wife Ida came about 4:00 to invite us to drive around town to see what there was to see. There was still scant traffic and many wrecked cars were to be seen, left crushed and helpless on the site where the accidents had occurred. There being no garages open or wrecker services available, and the occupants having been rushed to first-aid stations, there was nothing to be done for the cars but let them wait to be recovered when services could be restored.

One heard the radios blaring out into the street, giving rebel leaders' frenzied commands, instructions, and warnings. The majority of the folk parading up and down sidewalks was attired in rebel colors. By a stroke of luck, the only clean and ironed clothes I had today were red, black, and white, fitting right in with the day's apparel-color theme!

Rebel-flag arm bands are being worn by rebel soldiers, civilian militia, all policemen, medical workers, and former Batista soldiers who have passed examination by rebel authorities.

As we rode through Old Habana, we had to swerve around piles of debris in the streets where gambling establishments and the homes of *chivatos* had been ransacked and the goods thrown out into the street. Most of these goods had been burned. Little street boys rummage through the remains, taking anything they want and breaking up anything left partially intact. Such a waste of goods! The ones doing the tossing probably need these goods in their own homes, if they could just think about it. But of course that would look like stealing, so no one would consider it, I guess.

People sat in their doorways and on their balconies or meandered the streets, taking in all they observed, with the now-accustomed calm of the bystander. The lusty cheering heard only a few days earlier was gone, and every major intersection was policed by the militia—youth so young and tender in many instances that one wondered how they could support the weight of heavy rifles all day. No wonder they swaggered. Most of them seemed like very decent boys, though a few took unfair advantage of their new authority and power. Boy Scouts in uniform were helping to direct traffic.

The Second Front arrives in Habana:

On the evening of the 2nd, the Second Front from the Escambray Mountains in Las Villas Province arrived amid great rejoicing and celebration. They were a dramatic sight in army fatigues—their guerrilla uniform—and long beards and hair. Some had chest-length beards and shoulder-length hair. The hair length related to the length of their tour of duty—the longer the hair, the longer they had served in the revolution and the greater honor accorded them. They strode with a slightly hunched swagger, carrying rifles like a third arm. Many wore rosaries and Catholic medallions. Some had a hardwood piece on a neck chain which they had ostensibly inserted into their mouth to bite on during bombings in order to soften the concussion. (I believe that that was the explanation one man gave me.)

Others wore division or regimental flags thrown over their shoulders like a towel after a bath. Some still had an arm or hand bandaged. They were posted at main points around the city, and some got to ride in the classiest of new cars available in the course of their assignments.

The men seemed dead-tired that first day, having just finished one of the most-intense battles of the revolution on the 30th and 31st of December, and having been transported to the capital city in the next two days of continuous travel from the far-eastern end of the island to the other extreme. They happily received the enthusiastic welcome as liberators of the "People's Army," having suffered much and worked long for this day. The public watched their every movement, snapping pictures of them, availing itself of every opportunity to speak with them or be of service to them. This included many *Batistianos*, hoping to make themselves appear clean in the eyes of the victors. (It is said that many of these latter are already turning in their cohorts as *chivatos* and saboteurs in order to make their own record seem free-of-spot.)

Speaking with some of the rebel soldiers, I asked what they were going to do when this was all over. One wanted to return to ply his brick masonry in Las Villas, another, to his position as a foreman on a ranch in Camagüey. They seemed desirous of quickly returning home to life as they had known it up to when they had left. When would this be over? you ask. "As soon as things get organized enough," was always the reply. You query, "Is this going to be organized right away or drag on?" The confident answer was always, "Right away." "What will happen to the persons of the Batista regime who are still among us?" (The American Embassy had already received orders from Washington to not permit any Cubans into the States until authorities could be sure of the political leanings of the parties seeking entry.) "They will be tried, let go free, or imprisoned or killed if they murdered people under Batista," the former foreman from Camagüey told me. He described how policemen and soldiers in Las Villas Province had already been freed.

Fellow missionary Joyce Hill had described to us an incident of how this process had been handled near Santa Clara where she is stationed: A pair of Batista-regime police cars (they don't travel alone) was cruising around on the outskirts of the city. Passing a lonely country store, they turned around to stop a brawl they had observed brewing there. The neighborhood was swarming with rebels, however, who immediately entered the rustic building, disarmed the policemen, made them remove their uniforms, and rode them farther outside the city. They then let them out of the car—to walk back to town in their undershorts. This had the town rocking with laughter for a while!

We have heard tales, however, of how in Oriente province, they quickly killed police officers, having been storing up anger and resentment against them for these long two years of struggle!

Matanzas Side Trip:

At some point within these first few days after the flight of Batista from the island, a fellow missionary and I had to drive to adjacent Matanzas Province to attend some missionary business in its capital city, the city of Matanzas. Late in the afternoon, our work over, we got into the missionary car to return to Colegio Buenavista in Marianao. Just as we were reaching the Central Highway to resume our journey, Castro's triumphal army tour happened to be passing by en route from Oriente Province to the capital city, Habana. This caravan was composed of every jeep, truck, tank, and car available which could be scrounged from whatever source available, in which the rebel forces could be transported the length of the island to support Castro in taking over the command of the country. Every vehicle was jammed as full of rebel soldiers as it could possibly contain. Exultant crowds thronged every mile of the Central Highway the entire length of the island to cheer the troops on, throwing them food and flowers as they passed by.

There was nothing for us lady missionaries to do but to join the line of miscellaneous vehicles crawling toward Habana, and thus, it came to be that we were hailed by the crowds as triumphant rebels all the way to the national capital! We were two lily-white *Americanas* and not dressed in battle fatigues, but the encroaching darkness hid our identity. The public happily cheered us onward as part of the victorious army!

The caravan of miscellaneous machinery took more than two days to move from the eastern end of the island to Habana close to the western end. Castro himself was likely flown to the capital. His victorious entry into Habana occurred the next day, he atop a tank to greet the excited throngs. While it would not be characteristic of us missionaries to have made a trip into the city to gawk at the rebel leader riding into town, we just happened to be driving through the area on other business and chanced to witness his parade. I got a picture of him waving from the upper hatch of the tank. (See full description in Appendix.)

Missionaries seek to leave Cuba:

Sunday A.M. (January 4th): Barbara Smith, fellow missionary, decided on the spur of the moment that she would go ahead and try to get to Miami to visit her brother who had driven down to join her there. Pat Alexander, another missionary in Habana, had found out that there was a chance of her getting to take the ferry to Key West, en route home for a visit. I was the only missionary thin-enough to fit into the luggage loaded car to shuttle them to their respective points of departure. For two colorful hours we waited in front of the Hotel Nacional, Barbara's name on the list of tourists endeavoring to reach Miami by plane. She was number 121 on the roster. Pat's name was also added to the Key West ferry list. The American-Embassy-escorted convoy to the ferry left before the one to the airport, so Barbara accompanied us to the ferry dock. Later, she was able to board the ferry instead of taking her scheduled flight.

The militia, armed and wearing their revolutionary get-ups, waved the convoy on through at every point, and the trip went much faster than if we had been driving as individual cars. There was scarcely time to drop Pat and Barbara off at the dock, remove the baggage from the trunk, get them into the terminal, and turn the vehicle around in line before it was time to head back to the city and Colegio Buenavista. We were commanded to drive slowly so as to not incur suspicion or cautionary shots being fired at us. It is also helpful to be a "mere" American female at times like these, as we arouse less suspicion. We're expected to be sort of "out of it," being foreigners, etc.

Hundreds of American tourists were milling around the processing point at the Hotel Nacional, trying to leave the country. Five hundred had left by ferry the day before. Because of the national strike, tourists had to fend for themselves, having no food and being able to secure none or little. The Habana Hilton evacuated its guests en mass, turning over their elegant, glitteringly decorated establishment to the triumphant rebel army. Perhaps they had been commanded to do so by Fidel. One is made to wonder what condition this high-class hotel may be in after the tread of muddy boots, the touch of sweaty fatigues, the residue of burned-out cigars, and the hawking and spitting of the rebel rabble? The lower ranks are composed of country folk who know no better. Many of the leaders will not feel too out-of-place in this elegant hotel, having come from the professions before the war.

Che Guevara:

"Che" Guevara, Fidel Castro's right-hand leader, was an Argentinean with a medical education. On a motorcycling vacation trip throughout the Americas, he joined up with some Central Americans in their revolution. On a visit to Mexico, he met Fidel Castro while the latter was in exile there from Cuba. Together, they did a lot of the plotting for our Cuban "return to democracy and freedom."

(As alluded to earlier, it has later been discovered that Che had learned from the experience of other Latin American countries that if the Cuban revolution had attempted to establish a Democracy when it came to power, the United States would have found ways to crush and undermine its regime, as it did in Panama, Chile, and at least some 14 other nations to date. The only way to defend against that was to establish a dictatorship, as the United States' CIA would then be inclined to offer the nation arms, military training, a piece of the drug action, etc. Castro too quickly offended the U.S. government, however, destroying his chances of getting the military support he desired, so was forced to leap into the arms of the Soviet Union and China.)

Che has plans for taking 500 volunteers and going to "help our Dominican brothers to bring about their own liberation"—these words "from the desk of Dr. Fidel Castro Ruz, leader of the glorious Rebel Movement of the 26th of July."

Sr. Urrutia, who is now the provisional president since the military junta gave in to the strength of the general strike—it being supported by the entire country—has asked his Minister of State to bring the existing "dictator situation" of several Latin American states before the Organization of American States. This is a body which cannot and does not back up its recommendations and resolutions by police force. It must base its hope on the good will of the participants. Will Cuba offer its rebel army as a police force? Will Cuban rebel leaders wait for the dictum of the OAS before "liberating" the Dominican Republic? Or will its intervention cause other states to lose confidence in the OAS? If Che and Fidel go about the hemisphere "liberating" other nations, this would equate to unprovoked aggression. Trujillo of the Dominican Republic is heavily armed with U.S. armaments and equipment, as well as being endowed with American-trained strategists, as Batista had been—more of the U.S.'s "defense against Communism in the Caribbean." It hardly seems possible that Castro's army is strong-enough to accomplish the mischief outside Cuba which they apparently are dreaming of doing! (However, years later they did do just this in Angola and other nations in Africa. It seems likely that this was a make-work program to give Cuban youths something to do with their time and get them off the national scene, since there was not enough economic development on the island to employ all those who needed work.)

Once the revolution triumphed, Fidel ostensibly began to feel that Che Quevara was interfering in his control of Cuba—at which time, Che was sent to Bolivia to drum up unrest and stay out of Fidel's hair. It is known that Che died in Bolivia, reputedly at the hands of the CIA.

Aftermath of Batista's flight; the national strike; the sacrifices of families:

American news photographers are all over Habana now. They took shots of our ferry convoy yesterday. I have a feeling that they, in general, are quite naive in this scene. But then, we all seem pretty dazed still. Even the rebel soldiers act like they are not yet sure that it isn't all a dream.

One soldier was complaining about how willing everyone is now to get on the band wagon and wear an armband and carry a gun. "Where were they all this time when we needed them in the hills?" he blurts out.

But then, he didn't know of the quantities of our Habana youth who escaped from parents and schools to join up with the rebels. And he isn't aware yet of what the families had to go through when their sons and daughters left or were suspected of rebel activity—police ransacking their homes in the middle of the night in search of suspected rebels and rebel activity, interrogations in police stations, spies being placed to keep continual watch over their every move, innocent people being tortured, etc.

And he doesn't know why the strike didn't go off earlier in Habana as planned. The capital city was criticized by the rest of the country for not having an all-out strike. However, the dictator's policemen were everywhere stationed on the ready to drive the busses, watch workers in the electric and water utilities companies, and keep an extreme vigil over all. Guns were distributed to employees with instructions to shoot anyone who started to leave his job. New anti-strike laws were pushed through the rubber-stamp congress, and all employees were under strict orders to turn in the names of any fellow workers who didn't come to work. A few unfortunates were brutally tortured as examples of what would happen if others didn't show up for work. The bridges and important junctures about the city were under increased military guard, machine-gun in hand, fingers on triggers.

The moment Batista fled, this control was automatically lifted. As soon as the police guards were relieved of the dictator's command, workers went on strike immediately, as they had been hankering to do for a long time. The release of the six-year tension was tremendous! This is why we are still a bit dazed. And why the nation is at the rebels' feet in gratitude. And it somewhat explains the shooting and crazy driving and hollering in the streets. It partially explains the ideals looming so large in everyone's minds. These dreams seem reality already in the dreamers' minds, though almost nothing is accomplished yet toward a new national way of life.

To what degree can a new life for the nation come about with this broken-apart country, a dry treasury, a slap-happy population, and a completely new and inexperienced cabinet and government officials? And will we ever experience democratic elections?

The value of ideals:

The rebels won because they were fighting for an ideal. Batista could not win because his people fought for a mere salary. Can the new regime remain faithful to its ideal? The country has great confidence in Fidel—because they want to. Even at the depths of the revolution, people would still be prone to say, "I hate Batista, but we need a s-t-r-o-n-g leader!" Perhaps they have gotten what they wanted!

American "intervention" in Cuba:

January 19, 1959: Things have come to a high pitch of excitement lately over what portends to be "American intervention in Cuba." U.S. Senator Wayne Morse and Representative Hayes have questioned the new regime's hastily organized and carried-out mass trials, executions, and burials of the persons who formerly carried out Batista's oppressive orders, which are now taking place here. Can these "trials" be any less sinister than Batista's horrors, we exclaim!

Castro, in one of his appearances in public (this time at the Lion's Club) shouted at the U.S. to "Mind your own business and permit justice to be carried out in due course!" He stated that "at all costs, this justice" was to be administered "to the criminals —even at the cost of all trade with the U.S., and at the cost of a U.S. Marine invasion!" Remember, Castro was schooled in law. He had learned to control the mobs of people by his effusive rhetoric and fear mongering!

Ship leaving Habana harbor. The old Moro fortress protects entrance to harbor.

"There will be 200,000 dead gringos!" he threatens. "We'll make trenches in the streets and fight until the last man—even if it means all 6,000,000 of us!" he rails. As he was pouring out these invectives, there happened to be three U.S. naval ships at sea near Cuba which were expecting to put in at Habana Harbor on a routine maneuver, but when they heard of the possible military confrontation which awaited them here, they changed course immediately and steamed out of the area.

Military tribunals to quickly bring "justice:"

January 21, 1959: Sen. Morse points out that the way the Cuban trials are being carried out does not permit justice to be done. The trials are being handled in short order by militia—not judges or adequate juries. He rightly labels it a blood bath.

According to what we read in TIME magazine, some are not even given a trial. However, the firing squads may be an improvement over the blood bath that would have ensued if the matter were left in the hands of the public to "administer justice."

Raúl Castro and wife Vilma Espín attend Methodist dinner at Candler College to receive a Bible as a good-will token to the new revolutionary government. Raúl's involvement with the firing squads or the Communist philosophy was not known to the churches or the public at that time.

We had been fearing greatly the aftermath of the triumph of Castro over Batista, as so much desire for vengeance had been building in the minds of combatants on both sides! What we didn't think about in advance was that the show of commanding rebel power would have scared retaliation out of the thoughts of the vanquished. The victory of the M-26-7 (Movement of the 26th of July, Castro's army) had been so immediate and absolute that there was no opportunity for most of Batista's underlings to flee or organize to strike back.

Control in times of crisis:

This degree of a show of power appears necessary in times of crisis to maintain order. Ever since the administration of Franklin D. Roosevelt, virtually absolute power is now granted to the President of the U.S. in times of war and national emergency, which Cuba will feel free to emulate. But must it be so complete and so awful as in these Castro firing-squad killings?

One must wonder whether Democracy can ever take root from this sort of a beginning! I have not thought it possible, believing that it is an end which must be developed carefully by skillfully planting the seeds, watering and tending them gently, mistakes being accepted by all, and changes of course being made as needed. But, since after the first flush of rebel victory things seemed so rosy, I found myself initially questioning my pacifist ideas regarding the results of violent and hurtful means. Democracy seemed entirely possible to the listeners of the words of the new leaders, glowing with "vision, good will, justice," etc.

One totalitarian government supplants another:

January 19, 1959: Today, the way the situation stands, Americans here feel fearful. Or anyone with an opinion contrary to Castro's dicta on things would certainly never dare speak it! Missionary Betty Schafer remarked, "You are more afraid to say what you think now than before the revolution!" In other words, we are currently under a dictatorship as all-encompassing as we ever were under Batista.

Returning to the U.S.-intervention question, when it arises in conversations here, the fact that Batista's murderous actions were not called down officially by the U.S. government draws inflamed retorts from Cubans. From the point that this is mentioned in conversation, intelligent, logical repartee then becomes impossible. Somehow, the neglect by the U.S. to challenge Batista on his dirty work leads to Cuban justification for the mock trials and immediate firing squads being employed presently by the new regime.

It seems right to me to condemn the official U.S. condoning of Batista's ruthless acts—and it seems right to decry the sham justice that is taking place presently! They are not mutually exclusive or opposites. There is no need to argue them from opposing positions! But that is usually what happens when the topic comes up in talk with people. In any case, the U.S. government wasn't in a position to depreciate Batista's regime, as it was supporting it at every level to "protect our interests in the Caribbean!"

Our American government lagged far behind other nations in recognizing the power vacuum left by Batista when he fled and in acknowledging the new regime of Castro. This is a sore point for Cubans. This is the twelfth violent change-over of government in Cuba's bloody history!

Castro ready for establishing new government:

Castro hadn't missed a trick in giving a running start to the incoming regime! There were ambassadors already within most large capitals of the world to present the new Cuba's credentials to the heads of state and to introduce themselves as the representatives of revolutionary Cuba. Reports came in over Radio Rebelde during the first few days after the revolution's triumph, informing the public as Japan, Peru, and others accepted the ambassadors, thus recognizing the budding island nation. The one Cubans most wanted to hear about, however, was the United States' recognition. To not get it hurt national pride—and Castro's as well.

Fidel Castro is the spokesman for the entire revolutionary movement, especially now that he is seated in Habana. After having driven himself for three weeks on virtually no sleep, holding meetings until the early hours of the morning, he is now talking *"disparates!"* I.e., he is just running on nervous energy and speaking nonsense. He is inviting reporters and observers from all over the world to see for themselves how perfectly and optimally everything is running in the new Cuba.

Postal rates are reduced, parking meters are being removed (those which remain after the first exultant days of the revolution when mobs hacked them down), all is joy and peace. I wonder how there will be funds to deliver the mail and how the streets will be maintained if these things make no contribution toward these services. Revenue is needed to accomplish these things, isn't it?

The invitation to world observers was extended by the revolutionary leader after he had initially jeeringly and publicly invited Sen. Morse and Rep. Hayes to come personally to witness the "justice" being done in the new Cuba. Morse and Hayes had dismissed the gesture as "ridiculous." Granted, Castro had shouted his invitation at them in hurt and anger. Their clamor ceased, however, after his invitation. It is doubtful that they would come! Frankly, the whole picture is waxing ridiculous.

Castro begins his mass meetings:

Today, cars circle through the streets of the city with speakers blaring invitations to a rally, urging the public to attend the mass meeting of an expected half-million people in front of the Presidential Palace to hear and see Fidel. Hoards of the public accrue from all the provinces in order to take part in the "demonstration of support for Dr. Fidel Castro Ruz." Schools and all businesses (except the electricity and water works) are having a holiday today for this occasion. They are all as anxious to please this government as the last one, although there is still somewhat more willingness and spontaneity on the part of the public with this one, even though we are being just as coerced into opinions and ways of doing as under the previous government. It seems that people are still living on HOPE.

How free is "free?"

You can't merely decide you'll have a democracy and therefore you then have it! You cannot change overnight long-held ways of believing and doing. The greatest enemies of freedom here are the pressures on the public to get into the in-group (in with the government) and the penchant for those who enforce the law to be above the law. E.g., the men in olive-drab fatigues now drive down the wrong side of the street, turn left where they are not permitted to, etc.—doing just what Batista's commandos did when they had the power to do so in their hands—seeing freedom as the ability to do anything you want to when you are on the winning side and in power. It seems to the victors that the world now owes them glory and favors, something the rebel country folk have never experienced. It is obviously very heady stuff to the men in combat gear!

Attitude towards freedom affects students:

It is difficult to maintain discipline in our school these days: "We are free now!" the students exclaim. Also, the Second Front, made up of Habana University students, now demands recognition of their glory and sacrificial service to the cause "in the mountains," by invalidating the last two years of studies of those who remained in their universities instead of fighting. According to their plan, however, they are willing to concede that the high-school students (*Bachillerato* level) would only lose the first semester's work, while university-level students would lose all credit for the last two years' work.

The Second Front also sought to abolish all private universities, leaving in effect only the three state universities (Habana, Santa Clara, and Oriente), but it seems that somehow it was finally decided that a few of the private universities could remain open.

To close all the private universities would mean that the work of our Candler College faculty members to establish the first Methodist university in Latin America during this political down time would have been in vain. They have been working without salary—working for an ideal, as the rebels have been doing in the *monte.* While Candler University is not to be put totally out of existence, its scholastic work during the revolutionary ferment is not to be recognized. They will have to begin again to establish credit courses. We can see that the morale of the student body and the faculty is under severe duress!

Candler University will stand to lose students to the University of Habana when it opens in February. This is partly due to the fact that many of the students who entered Candler were from the U. of Habana who wanted to take advantage of time being lost during the revolution to make headway in their studies when the state schools were closed. Though they may feel like their time has been wasted, they wouldn't dare murmur in resentment against Fidel. I did overhear some Buenavista (my school) teachers talking about their dismay over losing credits and their studies not counting toward degrees, because attending Candler during the inactive period when classes were not held has drained so much of their time, energies, and family budgets—a sacrifice they made in hopes of making academic headway. The University of Habana costs about half of what it costs to attend Candler, a private school in its embryonic stage. Will it have any students left now?

Remembering Mr. Armstrong:

February 16, 1959: I have recently finished reading NOT SO WILD A DREAM, the autobiography of the famous World War II radio news commentator, Eric Sevareid. This life story was very interesting to me, because I can remember as a tiny child observing my grandfather listening attentively to the war news every night as Eric Sevareid spoke it over the crackling air waves. His voice and manner seemed to me to be those of a good, manly, intelligent, and sincere man of integrity, even when I listened with a child's ears and understanding, probably on account of Grandpapa's respect for him.

Here's how I came to have this book in my possession: During my first year in Cuba as a greenhorn missionary at the

Methodist agricultural school near Preston and Mayarí in Oriente Province, I met and fell under the spell of the quaint little old true man of God who was pastor of the Jamaican congregation of the Methodist Church in Preston. Mister Armstrong was his name. The sugar mill at Preston was owned by the United Fruit and Sugar Company, which had built the sugar mill and every building in the town. They controlled every person, business, and institution in Preston. And while they probably perceived themselves as controlling Mister Armstrong, he allowed them to think that with such grace and elegance that he could truthfully function as a free man, we might say.

For some thirty years he had been preaching and lovingly caring for, and visiting his flock, with his umbrella properly hung in the crook of his arm, among the West Indians who had come to Cuba three decades ago to cut cane here. Mr. Armstrong had the meticulous way of speaking of the most courteous and refined of English gentlemen. His thin chocolate-brown face and hands made stark contrast with his spotless white suit and shirtfront. He wore the woven-straw hat with a black grosgrain-ribbon band that was the style in the '20's and '30's. Elderly Cuban men still wear them when they dress up. Mr. A. had a pair of pince-nez glasses perched on the thin nose which matched his narrow face, and his hair was the thinning white wool of the elderly folk you instinctively revere.

His manner was crisp and perky, as was his body, which bent forward and backward while he talked to you. He was so respected and was such an institution that when the head of the United Fruit and Sugar Company brought down from Boston a painter to do his own portrait, he had the artist also paint a portrait of Mister Armstrong. Mr. A. was proud of the honor done him by the Company in this act and hung the portrait on the wall of his living room.

He was 80-odd years old when I met him, but he had a sparkle in his eye and a sprightly gait which certainly did not give away his age. He was quick to tell how old he was, however, whenever the slightest opportunity would arise—so that he could say, beaming, how many of those he had worked for the Lord, and he would then slip in a little testimony of how good the Lord was to him, and then would utter words of thanks to Him for having blessed him so!

Almost every time I took a girl from a cane-cutting village to the company hospital for care or one of our students to the company dentist, or my first, second, or third graders from the cane-cutters' village on an excursion into town, I would meet him out visiting. He seemed to love to stop and chat. He would always ask me when I might be coming to visit him "when we could sit and talk a while." I guess he knew the trials such a young foreigner would have in adapting to a new country, new people, new food, new bosses, etc., and he may have wanted to counsel me.

He asked for my picture to add to his collection of photographs of missionaries and church workers. I suspect that he prayed for all of us whom the pictures represented. I gave him a copy of the shot taken for my Cuban driver's license, I think—one very unworthy of him, as I look back on it. But being the one who mostly took pictures of others, I didn't have anything else to offer him.

Mr. Armstrong called me "Dear Heart." Oh, you couldn't keep from loving Mr. Armstrong! He spared nothing to help people. His house was across the street and beyond the big green lawn of the company hospital where he visited the sick. On the front wall of the yellow house (All company houses are painted yellow, as it doesn't fade in the tropical sun) which had been allotted to him, he had placed a neon sign which lit up at night, saying, "JESUS SAVES." And there was either a Bible verse or the hours of services written in smaller lettering under that.

His large front room was lined with books. It was a library—not a living room, as most people make out of their entry room. People had been giving him books for many years. The first time I went into his house, he said, "Now, Dear Heart, I want you to have a book—any book you choose." I poured over them for a long time and had a hard time deciding between selecting ROAD TO SURVIVAL by Vogt and NOT SO WILD A DREAM by Sevareid. "Well, you just take them both along, my dear," Mr. Armstrong said. The first one seems to now be given away or permanently lent out. It was a book I had always meant to read. I had used passages from it for several compositions on conservation of natural resources, which I wrote in high school and college, and have read quotations from it in numerous articles.

I had kept the Sevareid book handy for several years now, always intending to read it when there was opportunity. But it was just one of those good intentions until September of last year when I decided to get on with it during one of the periods when the schools were closed down because of the dangers of terrorism surrounding us. It is a thick volume written in fine print. It is largely Sevareid's autobiography but also treats subjects such as war, philosophy, ethics, geography, and many things worth considering. I copied out a few of the many passages which seem to speak to our times in Cuba in the midst of civil war. Eric Sevareid saw action in all the theaters of WW II. It is good to travel about, in essence, with a good and thoughtful man and share his experiences, even if they are vicariously experienced. Had I copied out all parts of value, however, there would have been a bookful of quotations! I am glad I read this tome, thanks to Mr. A!

Mr. Armstrong and fellow Jamaican churchman during a day of visiting and recruiting in the countryside.

Mr. Armstrong died a couple years ago in the Preston hospital during the revolution. I was not in that part of the island when he passed on, due to the war's activities and my assignment in Habana province, but I know the funeral would have been well-attended by the people of all the social strata of that area. Everybody loved Mr. A., as he loved everybody. I'm glad that he is now dwelling in the happiness and perfection of the Abundant Life which he so deserves and so believed in, the perfect "crown of glory" for the "good soldier" who had "fought the good fight!"

DIARY'S END:

Some six months after Castro came to power my time as a short-term missionary in Cuba was up, and I was required to return to seminary for at least a year if I was to continue in the line of work I had been doing for my five years on the island. This I did, attending Garrett Biblical Institute on Northwestern University's campus, in the expectation that I would return to Cuba after the sabbatical.

The downward spiral into Communism which things seemed to be taking before I left the island continued its tendency after I left. The political situation became increasingly tense in general, but especially for foreigners. The trends seemed obvious by the time I exited my adopted home that summer (1959).

I had earlier sought to become a legal resident of the tropical paradise which I had enjoyed for this period of my life, quite prepared to make it my home for the future. But my applications for residency had not been accepted by Batista's government. This turned out to work in my favor, now when I was needing to leave under the revolutionary regime.

Authoress working with children in depressed neighborhood of Coco Solo in Habana area, planting seeds for a Mother's Day flower for each youngster.

Leaving Cuba:

People leaving Cuba after the revolution at first were allowed to exit fairly freely, taking with them whatever personal possessions they wished. But as time passed, goods in Cuba became more and more scarce, and the new government increasingly clamped down on freedoms. Those departing the island were allowed to take less and less, until ultimately they could only take with them the clothes on their back, a Bible, and a wedding ring. These restrictions have been held to for at least forty-odd years now—maybe even 50. All moneys and worldly goods are to be retained in Cuba in a futile attempt to prop up the failing economy. Clothing and house wares were redistributed among "loyal" residents remaining there. And I suppose that departing persons are probably still frisked to be sure they are not absconding with any valuables which might enrich the country's empty coffers or clothe some resident of the island, etc. By now, however, there are sure to no longer remain many such worldly goods to redistribute! Huge donations of used clothing from U.S. society now make their way to Cuba, Africa, and to every continent on Earth. Thus, contemporary Cubans may better cover their nakedness these days. I see on television that Cuban women wear scanty shorts and tops which would never have been considered decent in the '50s when I was there! Our cast-offs as well as the skimpy and revealing clothing that American women so nonchalantly have worn abroad for decades, ignoring local custom, have now changed female dress around the world to our least-dignified styles.

However, at the point of my departure during the summer of 1959, things had not sunken quite to the level of only being able to leave with the clothes one wore, plus a Bible and wedding band, and I was able to take a suitcase full of clothes and some moneys hidden in the lining of my purse to be deposited in U.S. banks for friends who anticipated leaving Cuba later. It was a very fortuitous moment to be making this move! Incidents were beginning to happen, though, indicating the direction that things were going to take, especially for foreigners. As my leaving date drew near, I was having dreams night after night of being taken prisoner by airport guards as I was passing through customs and not being allowed to leave.

And there had been a critical event which had occurred the year previous (under the Batista regime) when I went home to Florida for a summer-vacation visit, the memory of which made me apprehensive as I was trying to get out of Cuba under a new but increasingly oppressive government, for what turned out to be the last time.

The year before, we had been allowed to go through the boarding gate at the airport, get on the plane, and take our seats, as though it were going to be a routine flight. However, we were delayed by the tower. As the delay crept onward, there grew to be an electric tension in the air among the waiting passengers. We nervously sat and fanned ourselves for some time, perspiring in the tropical heat. A palpable, unspoken fear pervaded the steamy cabin. After an extended wait, authorities came on board and removed a passenger, taking him back into the terminal. We silently felt apprehension for him, even though we didn't know the nature of his problem. It couldn't be good! Who knew how many others on board might be under a similar pressure! By this time we were all wishing to get the heck into the air and leave political unease behind us!

Ultimately, we were given initial clearance, and the pilot cranked up the engines. These turned, idling, for an extended period of time, but no final clearance seemed to be forthcoming. After some fifteen minutes more of waiting, the pilot taxied us out toward the runway, probably having been given some level of go-ahead. We waited on the tarmac, propellers grinding, for perhaps half an hour more. When the pilot turned the plane around and taxied back to the terminal, not a word was spoken among the people in the cabin, but the looks of dread on passenger faces caused everyone's adrenalin to be kicked up to the highest notch!

Again, official personnel climbed aboard and this time removed a man and a woman from their seats. Again, we all felt pained inwardly for them, wondering what fate could be awaiting them—and wondering if there might be others aboard who were still to suffer a similar fate! We continued to sit in strained silence, until finally, fortunately for the rest of us, we were given permission to take off and head for Miami. When we finally landed at our destination an hour later, some of the passengers kneeled down and kissed the pavement! I felt like it myself, having experienced so much vicarious apprehension, but my wearing stockings and a skirt didn't seem to permit it.

I balk at accepting Kennedy as President:

When Kennedy ran for President of the United States after my return from Cuba, I had become so inured to high-flown ideals being bandied about in Cuba that I couldn't take seriously his presidential-campaign speeches—though the things JFK ostensibly stood for would normally have been what I wanted in a presidential candidate. It all sounded like mere rhetoric to me after Castro's frenetic gab—like possibly using ideals to get people to commit to supporting your program, and then causing them to do unconscionable acts. I couldn't finally accept John Kennedy as President until the "Cuban missile crisis" arose and was solved!

I'm responsible for almost asphyxiating the Carrazana family:

When I flew back to the United States to return to school, I left certain of my most prized possessions in the hands of Rev. Carrazana and his family up the street from Colegio Buenavista, against the anticipated day of returning to continue teaching in Cuba. The box I entrusted them with contained (1) My family photo album kept from childhood, (2) a stunning velvet Christmas stocking, lovingly hand-made by my Aunt Margaret and encrusted with charms and trinkets of personal and family significance, and (3) a collection of flyers and handbills announcing public meetings and activities put out by the Castro government as it came to power and developed, as well as news clippings and magazines as the regime took hold. I had dated each one of the flyers so as to be able to document the character of this regime as it revealed itself, in case it had turned Communist, because the world at that time was waiting with baited breath to see how the new Cuban administration would turn out. I had no particular destiny in mind for this collection of writings and papers, other than to see what there was to see in this process and have it on hand in case there was ever an opportunity to document a government going Communist.

However, the situation in Cuba continued to deteriorate after I left. The police would bang on doors and demand entry into homes in the dead of night, perhaps sometimes at random, generally in the small hours of the morning, to look for anything or anyone suspicious. The public became beside itself with fear. Thus, the Carrazanas said to themselves that they had better open that box of missionary possessions in advance of any police investigations, in order to know for themselves what it contained.

And well that they did! I found out years later when I met them again in Miami how they had disposed of these goods. They sent the picture album back to U.S. soil with a returning missionary to put into my hands, though it never reached me. I've forgotten what they did with the Christmas stocking, but it also never came back into my possession, much to the sorrow of Aunt M. who had spent herself so lovingly to give me a beautiful heirloom worthy of handing down in the family. But finding the collection of handbills, the Carrazanas feared for their lives if it should ever be discovered by the police in a midnight raid!

What they did was, they waited until nightfall, closed the bathroom *percianas* (wooden blinds at the window), and proceeded to burn every piece of paper in the packet and flush it down the toilet. In the process they almost asphyxiated themselves, since the smoke had no place to exit the closed-up room. They were not happy as they recounted the experience to me in Miami two decades later! It was certainly a lesson for me about the care that needs to be taken when you involve other people with your personal effects and property!

I enter seminary:

After a short visit with my family in Florida, I traveled to Evanston, Illinois and entered seminary as required by the board of missions, with a view to returning to Cuba after a year of study. I did not at that time suspect the varied turns my life would take after I left and that I would never return to that island of sunshine and lush tropical beauty, though I did fly over it en route to and from South America some years afterward. Anytime I flew from Miami, I always carried the addresses of my friends living in Cuba, in case the plane should be hijacked and we would have to put down there. (This used to occur often in the '60's.) But this never happened to me, and we have had to suffer the insults of the Cuban postal service—which means that our letters may not reach their destination in Cuba or Cuban letters get to us in the States unless they are hand-delivered by persons whom we know when they make a trip to or from the island.

Somehow my letters have seemed less likely to reach their intended receiver than other people I know. While this could be a paranoid interpretation of mine, my inquiries seem to suggest that there may be more to the matter. I have written to Fidel Castro several times over the years, now taking him to task for treating prisoners so ruthlessly or making suggestions for ameliorative programs. Assuming that he may have read any of these missives, Castro seems to me entirely capable of stopping all mail between me and friends in Cuba and vice versa, though probably any such decision would likely have been made by some insignificant postal clerk who enjoyed exercising his little power over s-o-m-e-body. It seems possibly safe to conclude that Fidel or an underling clerk may have thus interfered with any mail that I would send to Cuba.

I nowadays send three copies of all correspondence to Cuba: One goes via the post office, one is put in the hands of a missionary friend who travels back and forth on church visits from time to time, and a third is sent through acquaintances in Miami who may take the letter over when they visit or know of others visiting the island. Even with all this, I rarely hear back from anyone, indicating that they probably have not received these missives—or at least certainly not all three copies! It has greatly dampened my enthusiasm for doing much letter-writing to Cuba, as much as I would enjoy being in touch with friends and former students of our schools—though I am starting to hope that under the governance of Raúl Castro, now in charge in Cuba, I'm having better luck getting and sending correspondence.

Seminary paper on Castro:

At seminary our psychology professor assigned us to do a paper on some public figure, making an analysis of the shaping factors of his or her life. I selected Fidel Castro upon whom to make this study.

It brought to my attention much information which I wished I had had while in Cuba, as I could have understood more of what motivated (drove!) the man Fidel Castro—and perceived how any individual with that much desire for power is deranged in fundamental ways.

In fact, when one scrutinizes the background of almost any person in high places, one comes to see that most of them are almost certainly driven by a will to power and a certain warping of their inner dynamics. This became especially clear to me some years ago after reading a book based on a dissertation called A SEXUAL PROFILE OF MEN IN POWER by Sam Janus and Barbara Hess. It was perhaps the most illuminating volume on this subject—and any book dealing with politics—that I have ever read. It brings home to the reader that if only the rank and file of the world could fully understand the emotional aberration which occurs for the majority of men seeking high political office in this or any age, the recruits would have more courage to stand up and refuse to become cannon fodder in any war on any scale that any war-maker launches in order to accomplish his own personal ends! And seemingly, the wars are intended to accomplish only personal ends for those who whip them up! Of course such leaders couch their calls to arms in the most idealistic terms, urging the bloody sacrifices to be made in the name of some great cause or principle, quite belying the personal gain to be made for the leader. Study will show this to have been true from a Genghis Kahn, to an Alexander the Great, to the Caesars, to an Adolph Hitler, to a Joseph Stalin, to a Radovan Karadzic, to a Lyndon B. Johnson, to a Bill Clinton, to a George Bush, et al, et al, et al.

Non-high-profile and truly great human beings are generally quite happy living an ordinary life, devoted to family, friends, business or profession, etc. They have no inner pressures squeezing them to bend the environment and world out of shape in their pursuit of wealth or power. We presently are awash in a rampant global Capitalism shaped by the inner pressures of an infinite number of capitalists, pushing for endless goods and things, baubles, mansions, machinery, etc., etc., in order to make incalculable accumulations of wealth and fortune, fame, and public recognition, etc.

This sped-up world culture is, at bedrock bottom, derived from the fact that so many people in these and other times have had so little true inner satisfaction in life, especially during their most formative years. With so great a population having so few of their deep inner needs met, only a ruinous culture and national and international life can result. And it has! In earlier eras, the mass of humanity was so impoverished that it had to suffer its inner skewings in silence. Once there was a business class and a middle class, increasing numbers of people could begin to aspire to and accumulate goods and services—and ultimately aspire to riches and dominion.

Fidel Castro did not have an ordinary early life. His varied needs as a child were seldom if ever met by his family and those around him, just as an Arafat's nor a Hitler's ever were. It is sad, sad, sad that millions of ordinary people must die or be maimed in the service of so depraved a worldview, not once or twice but over and over again throughout world history! With this perspective, one remembers with total sympathy the saying used during the '60's, "What if they gave a war and nobody came!" That would be a day of true victory for the common people of the whole world!

FIDEL CASTRO: A CASE OF IDENTITY CRISIS

(This is the text of my seminary paper written on Castro, turned in on March 3, 1961.)

Introduction:

Little do we suspect the extent to which authoritarianism molds our lives, generally. We swim in it as a fish does in water. It colors our daily intercourse with petty nuisances, it is a threat to freedoms for minority groups in our own and other countries, it threatened the stability of the whole world during World Wars I and II, it has caused crises in national groups with which we are presently contending (in 1961), such as Laos, the Congo, Algeria, and Cuba. And in these contemporary days (in 2009), lands such as Iraq, Iran, many West African nations, etc.

Persons respond to an authoritarian personality on the basis of their own personal needs and inner pressures, often thereby being made unable to view the authority in a rational way. Every one of us has some prejudices, some things upon which we have strong feelings for personal reasons. These are not subject to logic and are treated illogically by the authoritarian individual or those who react to him.

We would do well to ask ourselves what has gone into the formation of the personalities who are instrumental in shaping these critical times in history. To what extent have critical times in their lives shaped them? How can and should such individuals be handled, especially after gaining control over a political situation? How can they be recognized as a threat to their world before they work themselves into positions of great power or at least before commencing to wreak the havoc they will eventually bring about among their contemporaries?

I admitted to feelings of ambivalence toward the man Fidel Castro from the beginning. When you study a person thoroughly enough, you cannot but uncover material which makes you empathetic to him, either through admiration or pity or both. On the other hand, you uncover his frailties, and willingly or unwillingly blame him for them when they have adversely touched as many lives as Castro has. Besides, he was a very vibrant, attractive macho kind of man. Virtually everyone responds to this sort of a colorful person and leader.

Neither Fidel nor Hitler nor Stalin, et al, was produced in a vacuum. And the Cuban situation was not born from one either. Were Castro the only force battling for ill, we could cast all blame upon his shoulders. But he has amplified onto the world screen certain problems which most people and nations carry within themselves to some degree. It is easier to study them projected big and outside ourselves for all the planet to see in such a highly publicized case, than it is to look within ourselves where we bury such problems from ourselves and the world at large.

Two of the sources used for this paper as I originally planned it have increased my ambivalence. Adorno's THE AUTHORITARIAN PERSONALITY was written at the request of Jews in America who were seeking to understand what produces the kind of person who would obliterate millions in concentration camps and who continues to bear them malice within the context of civilized society, such as Adolph Hitler did. In a word, an "outside group" views an "inside group" to see what makes it tick, but not without some resentment, hurt, and anger, for all its "scientific approach."

The other source, which has helped me see Castro with empathy, has been Erik H. Erikson's YOUNG MAN LUTHER (the Luther upon whom the Lutheran Church was founded). Here, a psychoanalyst views on an intimate level a great man in his youth, showing us Luther from the standpoint of his own compulsive needs. As much as we fear or despise the machinations of an Adolph Hitler, a Joseph Stalin, or a Fidel Castro, if we look at them empathetically, sympathetically participating in their personality-shaping childhood events through the same ones we have experienced (because we are all human beings and share in the vulnerability to certain basic needs and drives, especially in youth), we do not hate them—only yearn with them for a release from the demons which have flailed them onward toward becoming the warped personalities they have eventually become.

The numerous biographies of the Cuban leader and his revolution, both in English and Spanish, have portrayed him as a victim of a ruthless tyrant—the clear-eyed prophet and tender shepherd of his people. But let's take a closer look:

Biographical sketch:

On August 13, 1926, Fidelito was born the third child in a family of five brothers and sisters, or fifth, if his older half-siblings are counted. His mother was "employed in the house of Angel Castro," i.e., she was a servant there. His father was a well-off land owner who married Lina, Fidel's mother, after his first wife died. Of the seven offspring, at least Fidel and Raúl were sent away to school in Santiago de Cuba, the capital city of their home province of Oriente, to be trained in their grammar-school days by Jesuit priests at the La Salle School. When Fidel was fifteen (Raúl, fourteen), they were sent all the way to Habana to attend the largest boys' school in Cuba, the Jesuits' Colegio Belén. Jesuit schools were likely chosen on account of their reputation for being strong disciplinarians.

There was a priest at Belén, Father Llorente, a teacher and "older brother to Fidel," who describes him while he attended Belén: "In any game Fidel played, he had the instincts of a winner. He was undisciplined, but a leader, a boy who cared little for dress or dancing, with a *guajiro* (hillbilly) complex, preferring to hang out with peasants and waiters." (1) After all, the Castro brothers were of humble peasant stock, though born on a plantation/ranch to a wealthy father.

"...He always preferred to cultivate friendships among the humble. His special friends at school were the porters, cooks, and workmen there. (2)

"...Fidel was seldom on the honor roll, mainly because he hated Spanish grammar, but he excelled at history, and he was better-than-average in geography, science, and mathematics. (3)

"...He was on the debating team (even though he was shy). The adolescent dandies of Habana treated him as a country bumpkin. He did not dance well. His clothes hung loosely on his lanky frame. The girls liked him despite all that, but he did not seem to be interested in them. He studied history, civics, the new Constitution, and for no apparent reason, the military tactics of great warriors from Julius Caesar to NapoLeón, Lord Nelson, Cornwallis, and Robert E. Lee." (4)

He had a driving ambition to stand out, to star. At the Belén academy he had been at the head of his class in twenty-two subjects. He had pitched for the baseball team, starred in basketball, and set a record for the 200-meter run. Fr. Llorente remembered of him: "He had to be the best at anything he did, and he tried everything." (5)

Another observer reports: "Castro...was called a *'Loco'* by his schoolmates—the brooder, the complainer, the whiner who was always being wronged, while always being right." (6)

And then, Fidel arrived at the university in 1945. He had a good scholastic background, an almost terrifying flow of oratory, and a flaming ambition to use it at every opportunity for as long a time as possible. (7) He ran for student president of the university law school and accepted all the help he could get from the Communists. After he was elected, Castro denounced the Communists. (8)

He majored in law and was one of those who traditionally keep revolutionary activity alive in countries such as Cuba. He is remembered by opponents as a "professional gangster," keeping the rabble aroused and doing whatever dirty work was required by the revolutionary program.

He devoured all food available, had a voracious appetite, but the most important thing (for him) was to have talk with his meals and for him to do most of the talking. (9)

Fidel cared nothing for money, unless some politician was stealing it from the people, a good friend of his recalled. (10) On his honeymoon he had to hock his watch and wire home for money. During and after the revolution in Cuba, he demonstrated little concern for the cold facts of life, such as money, lodging, etc. Andrew St. George says: "Fidel's offhand way with money is symptomatic of the personal way he runs the government." (St. George tells of how Fidel gives $2,000,000 to a man on the spur of the moment to set up fish cooperatives. When he saw the fellow ten days later, he asked the recipient of the funds what he had done with the money. "It's still on my desk," the man replied. "Well, spend it, *viejo*, spend it!" was Fidel's impatient reply.) (11)

Castro participated briefly in a revolution in Bogotá, Colombia, as well as one in Guatemala—both by happenstance, according to Fidel's account. But there he got a taste of what it would be like to lead a revolution, since the mobs appeared to him to lack control and leadership—something he would so enjoy stepping in and taking care of!

Fulgencio Batista Zaldívar, president of Cuba during most of Fidel's life, entered Cuban politics twice, the second time in a *coup d' estat* in 1952. Being a young attorney at the time, Fidel Castro sought to bring Bastista to trial and oust him by legal channels—but was unsuccessful. Castro based his challenge on the charge that Batista had violated the Constitution of the Republic. But the verdict pronounced to him after the trial was that "the revolution is the source of the law."

In 1953, Castro led an attempt to take over the Moncada military fortress in Santiago de Cuba as the first step toward overthrowing the dictator. It was unsuccessful, and Castro and his remnant of supporters were given a skimpy trial and sent to political prison on the Isla de Pinos until May, 1955. While in prison, Fidel gave classes in Cuban history and planned a comeback. Batista, in a weak moment, declared an amnesty for political prisoners, allowing his unrepentant opponent to go into exile in Mexico, where he gathered men and arms in preparation for a *golpe de estado* (blow to the state) against dictator Batista.

In Mexico his forces underwent training, and the plans for the *golpe de estado* were solidified. In December of 1956, Castro and his men, journeying across the Caribbean Sea in an open launch called the Granma, landed in Oriente Province on home soil, and began the struggle to unseat Batista. After the initial on-shore fracas with Batista forces, it was said that only twelve of the 82 original troops who landed with him were still alive. This nucleus grew during the next two years until the revolutionary army numbered some 10,000, according to THEIR account. (Apparently, the numbers for Castro forces were inflated throughout the revolution by the reports of Herbert L. Matthews of the NEW YORK TIMES who allowed himself to be recruited by Fidel to be the public-relations spokesperson for the revolutionary forces. Anthony DePalma has now authored a book called THE MAN WHO INVENTED FIDEL: CASTRO, CUBA, AND HERBERT L. MATTHEWS OF THE NEW YORK TIMES, disclosing Matthews' role in dramatizing in the public's mind the Cuban revolution and in attracting volunteers from the U.S.A. and other countries to swell the ranks of this army. Ostensibly, when Matthews first came to interview the rebel leader, Fidel staged the occasion in the dark and had his handful of troops to march and mill around the scene in the obscurity so as to give the impression of being surrounded by a larger number of forces.)

Ultimately, through sustained guerrilla warfare, largely fed on Fidel's vociferous determination, President Batista was driven to the point of fleeing the country on January 1, 1959, after which time the revolutionary forces were able to take over the Cuban government.

Cultural context:

History, as we have known it, is sheer drama. (I'd personally like to imagine an undramatic history, an uncharacteristic historical period of tranquility, economic and political stability, and a time when laws and government worked together justly and peacefully for the benefit and general wellbeing of the nation and the world!)

However, Cuba and her people have just completed (in 1961) another act in Cuba's drama. The participants have at times known what parts would be theirs to play in the drama because of what certain symbols within the culture have come to signify. Let us examine some of them, for whatever it might be worth. (Freud taught the world to perceive situations such as this one through such symbols.)

Cuba:

Spanish and the other Romance languages divide the world into two factions—that which is feminine and that which is masculine. All nouns are either feminine or masculine. In a sense, the stage is thus set for an oedipal dance to ever be played out among the speakers of this language.

Patria, translated into English, means "Fatherland;" coming from the Latin *pater*, the root word for "father." Nevertheless, in Spanish *Patria* is a feminine word: *la Patria*. In the way that Uncle Sam stands for the United States, the symbol for Cuba is a woman dressed in white (signifying purity) wearing a red cap with a single white star (symbolizing sovereignty won by the blood of martyrs). She is eulogized and sworn allegiance to on every national holiday—and such occasions are numerous, given all the coups and wars which have characterized Cuba's developmental story.

Tales about how the national heroes defended her sanctity against rapacious onslaughts of tyrants and plundering nations are recounted at length and in flowery and idealizing language on these patriotic occasions. She is the figure whose honor must be defended, struggled for, cherished, loved, and always thought of in idealized terms, in the same way that Mary, the mother of Jesus, and womanhood are conceptualized in Cuba and many other places where Catholicism has a strong influence. (Not that this religion was predominant in Cuba, as it has traditionally been overpowered by African animistic religion and in more recent times by Protestantism.) But the Roman religion, with its ever-present man on the cross, is influential-enough that the closing line of Cuba's national anthem is: "To die for the *Patria* is to live!"

Cuba then becomes the mother symbol, a strong, womanly figure of supreme value, especially if one's own mother does not fulfill the role which the son wishes she would. Fidel (and Raúl) lived only the earliest years of their lives in the presence of their mother. Perhaps she was in accord with their father in sending them away from home to be reared in institutions, or maybe she was (as in the case of Hitler and other brutal leaders) a mere frozen bystander while the father violently exercised his fears and apprehensions against his son through beatings and verbal abuse.

This father had reason to keep Fidel at arm's length—because, it was said, Fidel had organized the workers on Angel Castro's plantation to rise up in defiance against him while Fidel was still only a boy—before he wore shoes yet, it was reported by an observer.

What did Fidel think of his mother? Our only clue is that after he came to power, when she journeyed the length of the nation to the capital to plead with Fidel not to give away the family lands to the agrarian-reform program, he gave them away anyway.

A New York psychiatrist and friend of Castro's said that his mother, "I suppose, rejected him. Likewise, his father. This still disturbs his relations with other people on a personal level. It makes stability a difficult thing to achieve, when anything permanent, anything established or ordered, must remind him of childhood's emotional disappointments. ...It is my suspicion that his mother refused to breastfeed him." (12) (This is doubtful, as breastfeeding was universal in Cuba, and has always been in rural cultures around the world, surely and especially in this case of a peasant, uneducated woman servant. FCE)

"The tyrant:"

If one examines Castro's speeches and writings, they will find him almost never speaking of Batista by name—rather, "the tyrant" is spat out with vehemence, or "that monster," and other titles of disdain. Most of the population of Cuba was *conforme* (went along) with Batista during his tenure in office. Of course they did not like his breaking into the government as he did, and they would have preferred that he not filch from the national treasury—but, "oh, well," (shrug). Almost all Cuban history is replete with governmental corruption, a trait well-honed in Spain and brought by the conquistadores to the New World. The common people of Cuba have hardly, if ever, known anything different.

An examination of history of this period reveals the active part Fidel took in whipping up indignation against the "murderous tyrant." This was his revolution, his personal battle against Batista. Because of Castro's persistence and bitter resistance, Batista felt himself forced to become stronger and more vicious, retaliating increasingly and with fewer and fewer scruples. Here was the "father of his people" (as Batista saw himself) trying to discipline an unruly son and bring the family (Cuba) under control.

Castro was symbolically attempting to get back at the/his father. The New York psychiatrist mentioned above said of him, "He is a deeply anxiety-ridden man, very fearful of rejection, a syndrome that seems to go back to his earliest childhood, when his father Angel reportedly neither accepted nor acknowledged him." (13)

Remember, Fidel and Raúl were illegitimate and the offspring of a lowly serving maid. Angel Castro had legitimate progeny to be concerned with and more weighty matters on his mind, as he expanded his properties and plied his vocation as landowner and farmer. In addition, Angel Castro was a Spaniard, for-sure steeped in authoritarianism and a remnant of the hated Spanish yoke which had subjugated the resource-rich island for many years. This would not be lost on a boy who became obsessed with history as he grew up under his circumstances.

The elder Castro conceivably tired of the upstart qualities in his illegitimate descendant and sent him away to boarding school in order to be rid of the problem. Batista sent him off to prison and into exile, in order to be free of his sting. While Fidel was a child, there was nothing for him to do but to obey his father. His father "out-powered" him. When Fidel sought to unseat the dictator Batista, the latter declared immunity, because the power he had earned and had used to get into office made him "legally immune."

Castro was thus frustrated at every turn in his bids for power! For him, then, this was to become a combat to the finish! Neither man would give in until the other was exterminated.

During the revolution, when the tension and bloodshed of the battle was beyond endurance, civic groups, other elements of the counter-Batista forces, and the U.S. Embassy and government all endeavored to call a halt to the conflict and have internationally proctored elections—but the two combatants could not agree to it for first one reason and then another, so determined they each were to fight it out and become the victor. The winner's prize would then be the maiden Cuba; and she would be the winner's to have and to hold. The one could not enjoy her while the other was alive.

As Erikson says, the tragic thing of any ideological leader is: "He ha(s) raised human consciousness to new heights, but he ha(s) also to settle a personal account by provoking a personal accounting, ha(s) treated the universe as a projected family." (14)

When Fidel was told the news that Batista had fled Cuba, he seemed to have felt that he had been foiled again, and the tyrant-father had escaped him. He shouted, "This is cowardly betrayal! A betrayal! They are trying to prevent the triumph of the Revolution." (15) While this doesn't quite make sense, whatever it meant to him, he experienced it as something below the belt, and he felt cheated. It took the glory from having been left with the winner's spoils.

As a sub-point, since the source of the tyrant's power was the military aid received from the United States, in Castro's mind, every vestige of that power must go! Thus, the nation to the north became the father-power to the revolutionary leader. Castro seemed at times willing to take on that country—no, determined to take it on and conquer it. Or, if not conquer it, he would die trying. He needed an object toward which to lance his hostility, or otherwise he would have to turn it back on himself. To keep from seeing his real self (the one which repulsed his most-loved ones, and therefore, himself), he needed to maintain the hate campaign upon which his whole program is based—kill the father figure!

The revolution:

The revolution was the play itself. This is where everyone could get into the show and act out his own conflict, project his own hostilities onto something outside himself. Since it so strongly symbolized the struggle of good (Castro) against evil (Batista/the U.S.), anything the one side did was justifiable and acceptable, and anything the other side did was heinous and despicable.

Therefore neither opponent could see his own faults, neither could see the evil of his terrorism as it hurt innocent persons. The important thing was the principle of being the star around which the drama revolved! There was enough fact in the struggle for everyone to intertwine his fantasies, unresolved conflicts, and mind-sets into it, thoroughly justifying himself in doing so. Batista was just maintaining order, protecting himself; Castro was merely defending the people against oppression and demonstrating himself the innocent victim of an insane dictator/father.

The revolution provided magnificent opportunity for what Edmund Bergler calls "injustice collecting," the habit of teasing an enemy to lash out at a spoiler so that he can become a victim and all the fault be placed upon the other party. This justifies one's hating of the enemy. Hearing what Castro said at his trial after the Moncada attack, you can see how he views the dictator as a personal offense:

"If I have had to assume my own defense before this court, it is for two reasons. One: because I was practically completely deprived of defense, otherwise." (He actually chose to be his own defense. No doubt he did not trust anyone else to adequately present his case, but most likely, he would never forego an opportunity to do as much talking as possible and maintain as high a profile as possible at all times!) "The other: because only one who has been hurt so deeply and who has seen the (*Patria*) so forsaken and justice so vilified can speak on an occasion such as this with words that may be blood of the heart and entrails of the truth." (15) (Extremely dramatic and poetic words!)

The women:

The women filled the roles indicated for them. Mothers and girls identifying with that (protective) role, marched in demonstrations against Batista (which only women and mothers could have gotten away with in that era), visited the prisons to take food and other necessities to unknown revolutionary boys, as their mothers would have done if they had been near-enough to do so. They were instrumental in stirring mother instinct in the populace. By fomenting sentiment, they could participate in the strongest source of power. And because they were women, they could taunt the dictator to his face with relative impunity. A number of young women actively participated in the battles of the revolution, finding equality with men in a way new to Cuba. Fidel showed them their role: "Had (the original attack against the military fortress of) Moncada been successful, even the women of Santiago would have taken up arms."

Back in his trial after sixty-odd days in solitary confinement, Castro is grimly determined and feels more rejected than ever: "Forces gather in my breast the lonelier I feel, and in my heart is the desire to give all the heat that the cowardly souls (Batista forces) deny me...I listened to the dictator...from a shack in the mountains... Those who have not passed through similar moments will not know the bitterness and indignation of life. At the same time that our hopes, so often cherished, for freedom...were dashed to the ground, we saw the despot rise more braggart and worse than ever." (16)

As the book jacket of FIDEL CASTRO by Jules Dubois says: "Make no mistake, it was Fidel Castro's ideals...that inspired Cubans to spend their lives for their country, Castro's magnetism and indomitable optimism that brought men to his cause and re-invigorated them after setbacks and defeat."

Martí:

José Martí was the revolutionary leader in the War for Independence from Spain. He said and wrote many loved and revered sayings. He is the "Apostle," the Father of the Revolution, the national hero, the best-known poet. All political groups seek to found their ideology in him—making it publicly considered worthy of acceptance, truly patriotic. The lyrics of the popular folk song of the '60's, "*Guantanamera*," were verses of a poem by Martí.

Guantanamera*

Yo soy un hombre sincero de donde crece la palma, (2) y antes de morirme quiero echar mis versos del alma.	I am a man of sincerity from where the palm tree grows, and before I die, I want to sing out the verses of my soul.
Refrán: Guantanamera, guajira guantanamera. (2)	Refrain: Girl of Guantánamo, country girl from Guantánamo. (2)
Yo quiero cuando me muero sin patria, pero sin amo, (2)	I want, when I die, without a country, but free of an overlord, (2)
tener en mi losa un ramo de flores y una bandera.	to have on my gravestone a bouquet of flowers and the flag.

**This song may be from a musical genre descended from the Spaniards called "décima." The content of the refrain may have nothing to do with* *the words invented by the poet, as in this case. These are but two verses from the many written in this poem by patriot José Martí. This song was popularized during the '60s and '70s by Pete Seeger and other folk singers who rendered it in Spanish.*

Martí's name is invoked and his words recited at every patriotic occasion, from school presentations to political addresses. (Appeal to authority is absolutely necessary in an authoritarian society and an authoritarian educational system.)

Brennan, telling about political oratory in the university when Fidel was a student there, describes it thus: "Patriotism for Cuba was the central theme of every group. No speaker would mount his soapbox without a reserve of lofty language praising the glorious revolution against Spain, the heroism of José Martí, and the great heritage of Cuban freedom." (17)

At Castro's trial, he equates the ongoing of the (original) revolution (from Spain) with the on-living of Martí: "It appears that the Apostle (Martí) was going to die in the year of his centenary (1952 when Batista rose to power. It seemed to Fidel) that his memory would have been extinguished forever, such as was the affront! But he lives, he has not died, his people are loyal to his memory. ...Cuba, what would happen to you if you let your Apostle die!" (18) (I.e., if you forgot about invoking José Martí's sacrifice and leadership.)

In short, Martí is the idealized father image who died in an effort to preserve the dignity and honor of the beloved Cuba. In dying a martyr, he set the pattern for those who can never find resolution of their conflict with their father in another way. "To die for the *Patria* is to live!"

Ideological leaders should die at the height of their glory as a sacrificial offering for their cause. They then would live on in fame and be ever assured of the acceptance they continually yearned after in life but did not attain. The masochist obtains attention, love, compassion, even at the cost of his very life.

If ideological way-breakers survive the battles, they have the unpleasant task—and one quite out of their realm—of implementing their ideology in the cold reality of everyday living. Then is when the disenchantment comes. Castro is about the only big revolutionary leader of Cuba who has outlived the revolutionary struggle and been left "holding the bag" and having to implement all those promises and ideals he spoke of during the revolutionary period.

And we see the problems he made for himself. Being the originator of the movement, he could not compromise the ideals. Castro, Communists, and Puritans have in common a relentless conscience. In psychological terms, it is explained by their (lack of happy) relations with their parents. Fear of father, who was strong and perhaps violent, leads to rivalry and admiration for the father's power.

This puts a heavy burden of guilt and inferiority on all spontaneous initiative and on all fantasy. When a parent's actions do not fulfill the morals he forces on the child, the child can only develop a precocious conscience, self-steering, an obsessive mixture of obedience and rebelliousness. (19)

Now, he who was seen as liberator is more and more seen as a demagogue. How does it happen, again and again, that the best become the worst enemies of the good? ...The greatest advances in human consciousness are made by people who demand too much and thus invite a situation in which their overstrained followers inevitably end up either compromisers or dogmatists. (20)

Tortures and executions:

In a revolution, the followers identify with the leader and, in a sense, carry out his wishes unbidden. Whether Batista's men liked it or not, they were in the fray with him, and there was no turning back. Many had already gone too far and committed too many atrocities to be accepted by the other side if they defected. They were gripped in the until-death struggle, too. If Batista fell, it was their sure end, also. The innocents of the revolution were all neophytes in this sort of experience, driven by dreams of glory, and few had a "past." (Those who did were mostly adventurers freed from prisons in the United States who signed on in the revolution.)

So Batista and his men followed through on the fantasy by doing away with the masculinity/aggressiveness/"balls" of the son, incapacitating him so that his virility would no longer be a threat to the father. The variety of tortures employed in this war worked the macabre creativity that arises in circumstances of detention in many places before the Geneva Convention called for humaneness, but the worst of these during the Cuban revolution were perhaps those of emasculation. Rebels had their testicles lopped off or crushed. Sometimes these were placed in their mouths or pockets, displaying a perverted macho humor by Batista-ites, and these bodies were left in fields where they would serve as "a good lesson" to others.

It was even rumored by some of Castro's own men that he had been castrated by Batista after the Moncada attack, but I hardly think a man of his drive could be in such a condition.

Besides, he has fathered (many) children over the years by a number of women!

The son does not castrate the father, only kills him. Castro did not physically torture any of Batista's men; he simply executed them. This he called "revolutionary justice." Castro could not kill Batista himself, so he satiated himself by sending almost 600 of the dictator's men to the firing squad immediately following the "triumph of the revolution." When accused of unlawfulness regarding the execution of war criminals, Fidel's reply was: "There is a state of war in Cuba that is a product of a triumphant revolution. The revolution is the source of law." (21)

Fidel Castro had thus become the one he hated. When Fidel had sought to oust Batista by court procedure in 1952, Batista's court had ruled that he could not be removed because the revolution (Batista's) was the source of the law. (22) As Castro was denied a fair trial after the Moncada attack, he denied it later to Batista's "war criminals." The only difference was that Castro had enlisted others to join in his conflict and accomplished by popularity what Batista had to accomplish with what remained of his military and economic power.

The people:

Castro did what he did in the name of "the people." When he spoke of "the people," he referred to a mass. People for him meant "*guajiros*," country folk, the down-trodden. It was a collective term of an exclusive nature. That is the way he thinks of people—the good ones vs. the bad ones, the rich vs. the poor, the powerless vs. the powerful. He learned to relate to ideas and ideals but cannot relate to people as individuals.

But it is clear that he identifies himself with the victims—the poor, the stepped-on. Their condition makes them good—they deserve pity (cheap love). He won freedom for the people by shoving out the dictator; he won freedom for himself by shoving out his father-figure. This was the height of participation in community for Fidel.

Whenever there is acute danger, the impulse of most people is to seek out authority and submit to it. (23) If Castro could make the country seem a dangerous-enough place, the people could be persuaded to be on his side and help him extricate the tyrant.

The power impulse has two forms: explicit in leaders, and implicit in their followers. When men willingly follow a leader, they do so with a view to the acquisition of power by the group which he commands, and they feel that his triumphs are theirs. (24)

Jean-Paul Sarte put it: "The system seems to function this way: the people are confused; Fidel appears and tells the people what they want; the people decide Fidel is right." (25)

Who knows how many others in this situation were fighting out their oedipal conflict with their father, also! They reveled in the power that was theirs and the sanction and public esteem which became theirs as the revolution deepened. But this was primarily Castro's personal battle, which meant that he had to run the whole show. This was where he found a life purpose. He was saving everybody, of course, but since he IS the people, he was saving himself.

This revolution was won on a basis of *embullo*, a term Cubans use a lot to describe the dynamics of band-wagon-jumping-on. It was "the thing to do." If you were decent, you of course wanted justice and freedom; Fidel was fighting for justice and freedom; therefore, you wanted to be on Fidel's side and be decent. It became their holy cause transcending all other values. It pardoned all that would have otherwise been wrong. (But it transcended normal values because "the people" [in whose name the revolution was fought] is an ideological term quite apart from plain human beings.)

Since "the people" gave Fidel the acceptance he could not give himself, he felt whole and happy when he was with them, winning more of their affection, winning their approval. His hunger for popular adulation could never be satisfied or satiated! When asked why he did not get more sleep after the revolution triumphed, he answered, "My medicine is the people. I thrive on seeing and talking to the people." (26) In those days after revolutionary victory, the situation was so swashbuckling and romantic that everyone, no matter which side he had been a part of, was revolutionary!

The euphoria seemed unanimous and nonpartisan. And Castro enjoyed every minute of it—so much so that he worked virtually around the clock so that nobody would be deprived of an opportunity to talk to him. ...He seldom retired before six o'clock in the morning and only infrequently slept more than three hours. (27)

His mingling with the public stimulated and invigorated him. In each city where he halted, no matter what time of the day or the night it was, he delivered a speech and explained the purpose of the revolution and his plans for the future. He talked like a Robin Hood, and he never stopped until he had exhausted every point of argument to impress upon the people that everything he had done in the past and all he planned to do, was for their benefit and that of Cuba. (28) By getting the people's sanction, he could sanction what he had done. It made him and his triumphs all all-right.

In fact, since he embodied the revolution, an attack upon him was a blot upon Cuba and the revolution. See how this is apparent in the following words written from the Mexican exile prior to the revolution. In them, we clearly see the narcissism mingled with personal affront:

"I consider it my duty to defend my prestige and also pass judgement upon my opponents as I see fit. ...I have the right to defend myself because one does not devote one's life to a cause, sacrificing everything which others cherish and care for... just so that a handful of evildoers, who enjoy power through blood and fire against the people, for the exclusive benefit of their personal fortunes, can with impunity throw mud, slander, and shame against such sacrifice, self-denial, and disinterest, a thousand times proven to be at the service of a holy ideal. ...No matter how great may be his personal grudge, no dictator can afford to act against his own interests. ...The campaign of slander will earn its reply on a day not far off, in the fulfillment of the promises we have made that in 1956 we will be free or will be martyrs. ...When that hour comes (when the revolution triumphs), Cuba will know that those of us who are giving our blood and our lives are her most loyal sons" (29)

The people are an extension of him. If he is offended, they are also offended; if they are offended, he is also offended. BOHEMIA, then the most popular magazine in Cuba, carried an article during Batista's times entitled "Fidel is Not the Whole Country!" But embodying the revolution, Fidel bore the brunt of Batista's tongue continually and from time to time, drew criticism from his followers, who believed him to have deserted the revolution while in exile. This led him to write an article called "Against Everybody!"

But in every cooperative enterprise, the follower is psychologically no more a slave than is the leader. (30) When in the mountains, Fidel made a fantastic number of promises, and after coming to power he continued to make them. (Through them he needed to continue to cultivate the esteem of "the people.") And they were happy enough to have him solve all their problems. But even being active in his mission of mercy day and night, there came the breaking point: As people crowded around him to petition for prompt action on behalf of their problems, Castro told them: "I am not the government. I am not God! I cannot resolve all problems. (But he went on to say:) "They will be resolved, but it takes time." (31)

He wanted the right to act like a nobody but be treated like somebody, (32) but then there were times when he wanted to be a somebody but be allowed to be a nobody. Now he was finding out that to be The Leader meant to completely give himself to the cause and live constantly in the public eye. He could no longer show up now and then to lead a skirmish or to hide "below the radar" in the mountains. He must spend every waking moment fulfilling the ideal image he had become in the eyes of "his people," i.e., he must prove to the people and thereby himself, that he was the ideal, thus completely doing away with the real (bad-boy) Fidel. It was so terrible a demand that it hardly permitted him any rest, as though he had to keep watch on the ideal image to be sure it never lapsed back into the old Fidel. He could no longer live for himself; he was no longer himself, he was the idealized image.

Castro:

Castro became the long-awaited messiah, the one who would complete what José Martí had begun years previous. He was the new savior of his people. He embodied everything anyone aspiring to get ahead in life could want to be—educated, brilliant, apparently at ease and confident, handsome in a rugged sort of way, a strong bull of a he-man, adulated by everyone. His barbed tongue and humor made you want to be on his side and not the brunt of it. You knew on whose side you wanted to stand when he said things like:

"There is another reason that assists us, which is more powerful than all the others: we are Cubans. To be Cuban implies a duty, and not to fulfill it is crime and treason. We live proud of the history of our country; we learned it in school and we have been raised listening to talk of liberty, justice, and right. We were taught to venerate from an early day the glorious examples of our heroes and of our martyrs. (Theirs) were the first names that were engraved in our brain. We were taught... that you cannot beg for liberty but that it is conquered at the point of a machete." (33)

Castro was a master at manipulating masses. He controlled their brains, telling them what to feel and do. He intuitively knew how to play on the sentiments and what symbols to use. His speeches made almost anyone not committed to Batista feel down-trodden and in need of a liberator. Those who felt resentment could channel their resentment through Castro's world and words.

To illustrate this power over the public which Fidel wielded, I recall some years ago hearing a newscaster of very high profile (though I don't recall now who he was) commenting on Castro's sway over masses. The commentator had witnessed Hitler speaking before vast crowds in Germany as he was building his power over that nation. He had also observed Gamal Abdul Nasser speaking to hordes of Arabs as he called the Muslim nations to unite. But when this reporter saw Castro speaking to half a million people in front of the Presidential Palace in Habana, he had to exclaim that Fidel could mesmerize the people even beyond the ability of the other two well-recognized crowd-movers!

As mentioned earlier, many times one could hear from common people, while Batista was still in power and the revolution was trying to unseat him, the words: "Yes, we must get that monster out, but we need a strong man!"

That is, as it were, the "children" needed a "strong father" who knew what was right and could make them do what they were supposed to do. Everyone believes in doing the Right—if there is someone to make you do it. Isn't that what chaperones do for teen-agers? And police and soldiers and secret police—and dictators—do for the population? This way of viewing authority has been built into many Spanish-speaking cultures.

Father Llorente of the Belén school said that Fidel guided his men in a paternal voice (34) and: "The bearded officers and soldiers hung onto Castro's every word as he reviewed the past, present, and some of the future. Every one of his utterances was apparently both gospel and law to them." (35) This is the function of fathers and dictators in an authoritarian society—to lay down the law and cause others to conform to it.

Since Castro identified with "the people," in his description of the people he tells us something about who he is and what they mean to each other: "When we speak of the people, we do not understand as such the 'accommodated ones' (wealthy), the conservatives of the nation. ...We understand by 'the people,' when we speak of struggle, the great unredeemed mass, to whom all offer and whom all deceive and double-cross; who hope for a better and more dignified and more just Fatherland; who are moved by the ancestral desires of justice, having suffered injustice and scorn generation after generation; who hope for grand and wise transformations in all the orders and are disposed to give to achieve when they believe in something or in someone—above all, when they believe sufficiently in themselves, even to the last drop of blood." (36)

Chances are, working-class folk can understand exactly what he is saying, regardless of their nationality, while people who grew up in comfortable circumstances may have difficulty hearing it as something said of value. In any case, Fidel's style used playing and replaying significant word symbols, pronouncing and reshuffling them over and over again.

Yes, in Fidel Castro the people found identity, a cause, something into which to pour their love, energy, and hopes, something to cause excitement in life. No movie or novel could compare to the romance and adventure Cuba lived in those days! In the above speech, he has incorporated all the important symbols. All that gives meaning to the life of a "patriot," a "decent citizen," or a person at the bottom of the societal ladder—is bound up in those words which are taught every Cuban school child.

He would say to them: "These are the people who suffer all the unhappiness and are therefore capable of fighting with all courage! To the people whose roads of anguish are stony with deceit and false promises, we...say to you, 'Here you have it. Fight now with all your forces so that liberty and happiness may be yours.'" (37)

In fighting their revolution, the people were told by their leader that they were making world history. Castro would be not only liberator of Cuba but was going to be the way-breaker for liberty in all of Latin America. Those who were with him would then be of world importance. Through Fidel's prodding and prompting, they became increasingly united, determined that their revolution would shake the world. Since the culture provides for much idealizing and thinking in categories rather than in individuals and follow-through action, this appeared easy to accomplish and drew more and more followers. If they freed their own people, it was only a step away from liberating the subjugated Latin American and even African nations. Thus, Castro meant to the unfulfilled man on the farm and in the street, power, victory, meaning in life—a goal, and self-esteem. They acquired these feelings through his telling them how worthy they were, not because they had known how to come to this through personal development or action. It may have brought on a cheap personal development—yet raising people's sights and hopes is what a leader should be engaged in. Only by boosting aspirations might things ever improve.

He also gave them a means of getting back at authoritarian figures. They responded to his personality—but in an idealized dimension, rather than in reality. Che Guevara, one of the triumvirate of the revolution (composed of Fidel, his brother Raúl, and Che) made a disdainful distinction between kinds of adherents to the revolution: "(1) The fidelistas, idealists who follow Fidel with stars in their eyes, or (2) the revolutionaries, who had absorbed into their being the ideology, who know the party line, and were unreservedly committed to it," (as opposed to devotion to the man Fidel).

When we hear words such as these spoken by Che Guevara, we can understand why Fidel wanted to be rid of him, thus sending him to South America to foment revolution—where he ultimately was killed.

The Catholic Church

What the Catholic Church has meant to Fidel and Raúl and what it has meant to the bulk of the population are two different entities. And it has followed that it has been the point of rift between them which widened over the years after the Castro forces triumphed.

To the Castros, the church meant an extension of the father's tyranny. It was the substitute family which taught them the ideals they were to adhere to but which perhaps were not followed in a consistent pattern. But its main drawback was that it was an institution and could not give them the love, acceptance, and guidance which they needed from loved ones and their family as children. Remember, Fidel and Raúl were virtually reared by the Jesuits, the most unbending and demanding of the orders within that church. The Jesuits were that artificial family whom they likely sought to please because they had to continue in whatever level of family the Jesuits were to the boys—but whom they hated. And there was no feminine influence, something needed by all children in order to develop normally. The Jesuits, like the father, were always right, yet their lips always carried words of elegance and beauty to cover up the human frailties which generally lurk in such human conditions. Castro cannot accept the fact that he is a frail human being; he has to be the saint, the savior, at which point he would win the respect of the church, priesthood, school hierarchy, etc.

While, in the beginning of the revolutionary period after Batista fled, the Catholic Church was allowed to participate in public meetings as it traditionally had done and felt was its right, it soon learned that it was not going to be permitted the honored position it had held for centuries and now felt it had earned during the war years. True, the clergy had ministered to the soldiers in the hills, they had blessed the boys and thrown their sanction against the dictator when it was safe to do so—and even sometimes when it was not. But they quickly found where the power now lay. It was reserved for the very few in the revolutionary hierarchy and not for any competitors.

Wounded and resentful, and seeing that its main source of power, God, is not part of the revolution, Catholicism began a counter movement in Cuba after the triumph of the revolution. Into the symbol of the Catholic Church, the same struggle was commenced anew. There were those who sought to oust the new and hated tyrant in the name of the same Martí, Cuba, justice, democracy, God, etc. We see that they were not successful in this. Religions became disdained and curtailed by the now-in-power revolutionary government.

Prior to and during the revolution, the Roman Catholic Church meant to the populace a mixture of whatever was ideal, sanctified, magical, powerful, and revered. A deal of superstition and fear kept people in awe of the church, power, and God. The saints and priests were the point at which God touched the earth; they are the ones who worked the power magic. To fly in their face was a thing no good superstitious or religious person would do. The church contained what was holy and was not to be challenged by human understanding or taunts. When the revolution and the Castros showed themselves opposed to it, the church lost great numbers of adherents in that moment.

However, forty years later, Fidel Castro felt obliged to "eat humble pie," going to Rome to invite the pope to visit Cuba, from which vantage point, Castro hoped, the father of the Catholic world flock would urge the United States to lift its economic embargo (leveled against Cuba by President John Kennedy). Cuba at this point was starving and its economy in utter shambles after the Soviet Union had stopped propping it up financially.

For the first time in decades, masses of Cubans were allowed to turn out by thousands to hear the pope—the first time that worship could be held in public after its rejection by the revolution in 1959. In the films of this occasion, we see a Fidel, uncharacteristically humble, greeting the *Papa*, reigning himself in to attentively be present as one of the "faithful" publicly—before the masses whom he has for 50 years addressed by entirely dominating the scene—never sharing the limelight as he was here doing with the aging pope! Truly, nothing stays the same forever!

Other symbols used:

Since superstition runs rank among Cubans and many people in tension and distress, mention might be made here of some of those symbols in which people put their hopes during the revolution.

Numbers:

Castro was born on August 13, 1926. Twenty-six is twice 13. The ill-fated attack on the Moncada Fortress which, gave birth to the revolution and gave it its name, fell on July 26. The amnesty which permitted Castro and some followers to leave prison and go into exile was pronounced on the 13th day of May, half of 26 and Fidel's birthdate.

All through the revolution, rumors would indicate that a general strike or big battle was in the offing—but when? Since there was no source of verifiable news, the populace would begin to speculate: Would it happen on the 2nd day of the month? If that passed tranquilly, it would be thought to probably be the 6th (the two constituents of 26). No? Then the 8th—i.e., 2 + 6. Or the 12th (2 X 6)? Or the 26th, the anniversary? The belief in the number 13 was revolutionized in Cuba during the revolution. Whereas it had been one to fear in former days, now it was a lucky number. Who knows how many lottery tickets were purchased (and are still purchased by Cubans, even in the U.S.A., today) on the basis of numerical speculation like that!

The Dove:

Then there was the pigeon which came and perched on Fidel's shoulder for several hours as he spoke to the people on the eve of his victorious entry into Habana in January of 1959. Several of the birds were released from a box at the start of his speech, and this particular one flew across to sit on his shoulder. It was proclaimed the dove of peace, and of course seen as some heavenly designation of blessing! Busts of Castro with the pigeon perched on his shoulder were quickly mass-produced to be sold on the streets, along with other "revolutionary souvenirs."

To add to the seeming divine sanction, only twelve of the men who landed on Oriente soil as they came from Mexican exile lived to see the revolution come to victory. One of those was shot before they could reach Habana after Batista fled. There you have the "savior and his eleven faithful apostles."

The long hair and beards cultivated in the hills enhanced the illusion of biblical characters. They called Camilo Cienfuegos, a high-ranking leader, "the missionary." He seemed so visionary, mild, and holy. However, as the new government settled into its commanding role, one by one a number of the higher-up leaders outside the triumvirate (Fidel, Raúl, and Che), began disappearing mysteriously. One was killed in a plane crash, I recall, and others died in different "mishaps." However, none of these seemed to dampen enthusiasm for the revolution more than the death of Camilo Cienfuegos. After his passing, a certain despair began to set in like rigor mortis.

Then there was the added significance of the beard and hair length, as described earlier, how long they were indicating the amount of sacrifice and time given in "the hills" and the consequent prestige.

And so forth, on and on. In such "significant" moments in history, every detail becomes imbued with a certain importance which it might not otherwise have.

IDENTITY CRISIS

The revolution was the result of an ideology; it created an ideology, and has perhaps carried on toward a sequel ideology, all related. Erikson describes ideology as that "unconscious tendency at a given time to make facts amenable to ideas, and ideas to facts, in order to create a world image convincing-enough to support the collective and individual sense of identity. It exerts dominance on the seeming logic of historical events and by its influence, on the identity formation of individuals." (38)

How ideology came to revolutionize Cuba.

A person who is happy and fulfilled in his work and family is able to live an uncomplicated and simple life. His joy is serving his loved ones and mankind. As the great Chinese sage, Lao Tzu, said, a master (who has learned the disciplines required by life and is on the path to perfection) is "content with an ordinary life and can show all people back to (it)." (TAO TE CHING, reading no. 65, Stephen Mitchell translation) We know from studying the lives of highly ambitious people, that they are not content with an ordinary life. They must stand out from the rest. They must control people and moneys, and have a position of power.

An ideology develops because a person's needs drive him toward an identity crisis. They have pressing needs for devotion to something larger than themselves in order to be larger themselves—needs for repudiation of someone or something, needs for meaning, needs for relationships. They bask in the devotion that they draw from others for the great cause they are developing—which they weren't able to get for themselves alone. They cannot rest until they become hooked to some star which will put in motion all these forces. They are driven by their inner pressures. And ideologies offer overly simplified and determined answers to vague inner states and urgent questions arising in consequence of the identity conflict. (39) That is, the inner pain is too great to withstand without amelioration of some nature.

Thus, it comes to seem better to the individual in an identity crisis to put the attention outside the self—on others, on outside issues or ends, on far-away places. It thus seems imperative to cause a war on the other side of the world—than to keep attention, resources, and focus of personal attention on the inner problems or lacks of the self or the nation.

Youth becomes the initial and often backbone power in revolutionary situations, whether they understand the true issues involved or not, because of the driving force of these needs and the powerful, unaccustomed hormones coursing through the youthful veins. At this stage of life, a young person aligns himself with powerful forces beyond himself as a means of proving that he is reaching adulthood, the time when he may exercise his own power. The revolution or the gang or the platoon becomes his family, where he may acquire a feeling of unity, solidarity, or warmth, common bond, and purpose—at the same time he is needing to prove himself as an independent entity, his own man. We saw this over and over among the Native American young men in earlier days of our country who readily became a warrior to protect the tribe. There is no other choice, once the task is enjoined, for a man with the drives and background history of a Fidel Castro.

It proves to be at the same time intimately related to his most personal conflicts, his superior selective perception, and stubbornness of his one-way will: he must court (adversity) in order to test the alternative of whether the world will crush him or whether he will disestablish part of the world's worn-out fundaments and make a place for a new one. (40)

For a truly creative person, a new pattern is established. For Castro and for Cuba, the new way of life was the most radically different plan that could have been conceived—as consideration for the needs of poorer persons never figured in former Cuban revolutions—or those of the vast majority of other nations' revolutions. And it would have been a truly distinct revolution—except that the same old military machine is necessary to put it into effect when the son becomes the father and must now be the originator of programs, ideas, and methods when he must be the one to control the national way of life. He sacrificed much to arrive at this position, and he must maintain it in order to live with himself and the country. To face his inner despair, his hostility toward himself, the despicableness of the real Fidel, would be unbearable. It would demand a more world-shaking revolution—the one within him.

Such an inner revision could only occur in a safe relationship with an individual who loved and respected him and whom he could love without their manipulating him, who would not try to use him, who could accept him as he was. (The New York psychiatrist mentioned previously might have been the one person who could have been able to help him, but she fell in love with him, an inappropriate response in the counseling relationship, undermining whatever counsel she was able to offer him.)

Castro gave of himself to be used by "the people," because he believed that that was the only thing he was good for. He could deserve to go on living if he did enough good things and was therefore good enough. And the firing squad for anyone who thought that what he was providing for them was not good enough! He became the authoritarian father and wanted to provide for his nation of children. All he asked was that they accept what he gave them—and thereby accept him. He was driven to buy the people's love with the things he gave them.

Here is an identity conflict arrested in a pathological stage—because his inflexibility and strictness provide for more injustice-collecting, more vehemence, more executions, more resentment, more revenge of the populace, further retaliation, continued executions, etc. It can't be resolved and handled, because there must be an enemy against whom to cast the attention, thus keeping the nation united in devotion and attention.

How did it go wrong, wonder those who poured their whole fortunes into the revolution, those who lost loved ones, by Castro himself. All are bewildered by how things have gone so astray since the revolution triumphed. Castro had lifted his patient-hood to the level of a universal father figure and tried to solve for all what he could not solve for himself alone. (41) But it had to be solved his way—which was no solution. The abused child becomes the abusing father.

The torturous self-consciousness such as Fidel Castro has, keeps him wary of intimacy. Intimacy with another would arouse the impulse to merge with the other person and fear losing his autonomy and individuality. (42) He is caught in the paradox of need for intimacy and fear of intimacy. So intimacy with the entire country makes sure that there is no intimacy with any single (and scary) person—one who could wound him at the deepest level. Retaining himself and giving himself are one. This prevents his ever coming to terms with his identity crisis. The crisis is sustained, and probably will be throughout his entire lifetime.

We must note, however, that he did manage to have enough momentary intimacy with several women to have fathered two or three children in his youth and, in later years, to beget many children by one woman sequestered in a distant place. The press and public were forever kept distant from his personal life.

How much has negative identity played a part in Castro's personal crisis? Youths seem to search for total and final values, and they often find them in whatever is foreign to all they have been taught. (43) Fidel was of a landed and moneyed family. He later repudiated all such persons. He used their money and influence as long as they were useful to him and the revolution, until he could gain the victory.

"Fidel has unquestionably superior intelligence, good judgement, superb memory," his psychiatrist friend said. (44) He was well-educated, but those who came under his favor were those with little or no education and scant intellect, who would "buy" his emotional appeals to their scarcity of rational abilities. He was reared in a conventional religious framework—and he came to recant anything smacking of religion. Anything which was normally acceptable for a person of his background later became not acceptable for him. He threw off the old personal history and that which produced it. He created a new personal history, and everything and everyone had to conform to his idea of the new creation. He may have felt for a time that he had won the battle over the old and objectionable.

It is clear...that the negative conscience which had been aggravated so grievously by his paternalistic upbringing had only waited (as such consciences always do) for an opportunity to do to others in some measure what had been done to him. (45)

Ideological leaders are subject to fears which they can master only by reshaping the thoughts of their contemporaries—while those contemporaries are always glad to have their thoughts shaped by those who so desperately care to do so. "Born leaders" seem to fear only more consciously what in some form everybody fears in the depths of their inner life—and they convincingly claim to have an answer. (46)

We have examined here some of Castro's inner fears. While Castro gave the impression of fearing nothing, there could not but lurk down deep within him that inevitable residue of the real Fidel, the little boy who never felt loved, accepted, protected, cared for or encouraged. What is left of that little boy can never rest.

There are clear signs that Fidel is concerned with the prospect of sudden violent death—and there have been quite a number of attempts on his life. When one July the journalist Andrew St. George flew to Camagüey with him in his private plane, he (Castro) was startled by the sight of flames belching from the engine exhausts during warm-up. The steward tried to reassure him that this was a common sight, but Fidel was worried. He ordered the engines stopped and questioned the sweating pilot for ten minutes before he allowed the plane to take off. (47)

Not even his right-hand men knew from one hour to the next where he would show up. He might have been on the eastern end of the island in the morning, eaten lunch in Santa Clara (in the middle of the island), spent the afternoon running around Habana, and spent the night in the Ciénega de Zapata at the far western end of the country. Sleep was erratic, seldom ever in the same place successively. This way, he could keep vigil over the whole country and not permit anyone to "get at him." (And in 2009, we can see the toll that a life so lacking in healthful routine has taken on him.)

Far from being solved, the real, original fears are likely as far from being seen and coped with as ever. They could not but sneak out of control in these expressions of more superficial fears. And ultimately, they would manifest in health declines. And of course continual smoking of big Cuban cigars and consumption of alcohol over the many decades would relate to the quality of his health today in 2009. (He is said to have had bouts with cancer, lung, and heart problems, etc.)

The self-doubt would win out, no matter what. Self-doubt leads to more stringent demands for perfection. Being dogmatic with himself, he could not but be dogmatic with others. Erikson describes what happens: Leaders somehow know how to exploit our unconscious without understanding the magic reasons for their success; and consequently, their success contributes to their being corrupted by leadership. Dogmatic leaders are the worst, for they combine a moral scrupulosity with a deadly unscrupulousness, a mixture which permits them to take command of our conscience. They know how to dull our perception so that they can involve us in mythical realities which we can neither manage to believe completely, nor afford to quite disbelieve. (48)

(Erikson's words are about Luther, but naturally they apply in Castro's case:) (He) tried to free individual conscience from totalitarian dogma; he meant to give men creedal wholeness, and, alas, inadvertently helped to increase and to refine authoritarianism. (49)

The identity crisis is intensified when the masses respond. Their response commits him permanently to the cause.

The crisis of an ideological leader naturally emerges when he must recognize what his rebellion (which began with a more or less disciplined fantasy—to the political world in the widest sense) has done to the imagination, the sense of reality, and the conscience of the masses. (50) Castro quickened the sense of civic duty, the feeling of the necessity of doing "right" and "good," but became impaled on the horns of the same dogma. The tragedy of an ideological leader is that he exploits in all sincerity only to have his sincerity exploited. (51) Or, as the Chinese sage Lao Tzu said, "When the will to power is in charge, the higher the ideals, the lower the results." (Reading no. 58, TAO TE CHING, Stephen Mitchell translation.)

Post Script

History (now in 2009) has not yet recorded how Fidel Castro finally dealt with his identity crisis. However, after 50-odd years, the sands of time are slipping away and will soon empty the hourglass. He has survived many assassination attempts. He has heart disease and has had colon cancer. He is known to have fainted on occasions. Raúl, his brother, has lived a more conventional life than Fidel, and he has a ruthless determination and focused energy which may bring him a more extended lifetime.

Of course, the hundreds of thousands of Cubans who have gone into exile in Spain, Venezuela, Mexico, the United States, etc., have for all these years been expecting Fidel at any moment to come to some sort of an end which would enable them to return home to their beloved Cuba. He has outlived a significant percentage of them and most of them have fared infinitely better in their places of exile than if they had stayed in their homeland in the sun. They didn't think about the possibility of Raúl's assumption of power—until now, when it seems so logical.

The exiles have lived in the fantasy of returning home for a number of decades. But if they were actually challenged with the opportunity to go back to Cuba, the dream of it in their imagination would have to vaporize very quickly. These ex-patriots now have children who have grown up and had children in their adopted homelands. They would certainly not want to leave the relative plenty and security they have cultivated in their new homelands, certainly in the U.S.A.—in order to go to a small impoverished island that cannot even support its present population! The majority of their offspring are successful people in their adopted homelands. It would be such an abrupt break in the continuity of the exiles' lives and those of their progeny for them to now return to the Father-Motherland, that few, if any, would elect to return to natal soil for more than a brief visit. For them to do so would overwhelm the resources of Cuba, already foundering and inadequate!

To further fix them in their adopted homelands, the properties and businesses which the exiles may have held in Cuba before exiting have been given to others remaining in the *Patria* or have been taken over by the government. In other words, there is very little that former Cuban citizens would have to go home to in Cuba other than to revel in the memory of its beauties and warmth.

If they went back, they would be among the masses that have no recourse but to expect doles from the government or inadequate jobs which would compensate them with mere pittances—if indeed such employments might even be obtained. And very meager foodstuffs have been available at any price, anywhere there today. Robbery in Cuba today is rampant. It is said that families must always leave some family member on the premises when they go away for some purpose in order to protect their goods and home.

Scraping a living from the soil has caused farmers to return to the cultivating practices of their ancestors. Fossil fuels being at such a premium and mechanized, workable farm implements being virtually non-existent anymore, plowing and harvesting is presently done the original way—with oxen, muscle power, and hand-made tools. Thus, organic agriculture lives in Cuba! It is the Permaculture (permanent-agriculture) model for the world in this era of "peak oil." Citizens interested in farming available lands are allowed to sign an agreement, promising to till the soil of any vacant lots and unplowed fields, selling their crops in street stalls to the public at large. In fact, those who have become good at this kind of farming are contemporarily the best-fed and some of the best-well-off of common citizens living there presently.

Visitors to Cuba these days perhaps observe the once-beautiful colonial architecture in Habana, now in quite decayed conditions, and may even get to observe some of the exigencies which folk in the hinterland must endure in the course of their daily lives. However, the foreigners I have met who have traveled to Cuba for the quick look-see they are permitted, often do not comprehend the total picture and frequently leave the island feeling that the Castro administration has been quite successful in meeting the national needs. This is because they didn't observe this culture as it was fifty years ago when life was simpler but goods flowed naturally in a more productive economy—albeit under a dictator who had access to trade with the U.S.A. Life in Cuba currently is a struggle, but it is interesting to note how there is a spirit of "We're all in this together. Let's make the best of it!" which has perforce been cultivated there. Because of the fifty-year-long embargo which the U.S.A. has enacted against the Castro regime, non-Cuban Americans may not visit the island nation unless on certain serious business, such as church matters, or to take food and clothing to be donated there, or to make a movie, etc.

So some residual questions remain: How much longer will the Castro brothers live? Is the status quo so ingrained that politics will continue as usual after they go? That is, will the essential political structure continue as Cuban-style Communism? (Surely Raúl will see to it that it shall as long as he lives, though it must be acknowledged that some small reforms seem to be happening under his aegis. At least he has asked for public input in how to improve things.)

The present populace knows no other way of life than the one they have lived for these five decades. At a governmental level there would be little motivation to return to the early vision of establishing a democracy, given that the Neighbor to the North would not tolerate a sovereign, democratically elected government just off its southeastern coast.

Will the aggressive contemporary U.S. government intervene to more directly control the island "for security reasons?" It has been done in Pakistan and Iraq. Unless the Muslim world mounts a stronger counter attack against the United States' administration, thus ending American ability to go where it wishes and do what it wants, acquiring another "protectorate" for the U.S. to control could easily come into the American imagination, since the U.S. continues to maintain its strategic base at Guantánamo.

If such a United States invasion of Cuba should occur in order to acquire control of it, it would be like taking candy from a child, given the economic level of today's Cuba. If it should happen, a person's culturally informed impulse is to exclaim, "God help us all!" However, one who contemplates the matter realizes that God is hardly responsible for commandeering human beings to undertake political aggression or war and is not going to succor one group against another, since He is ostensibly Father of all mankind and would not play favorites (notwithstanding the accounts of this in the Old Testament). The best in Islam and Christianity recognizes this supposed equality under the parenthood of the Maker of the Universe.

Surely we can assume that God gave us this assignment so that we could learn to make peace on earth! This is a huge task, given that the powerful individuals capable of making war have acquired the armaments and legal apparatuses requisite to controlling the conditions at national and international levels, according to their greed- and power-driven wishes. Individual human impulses to garner political command, wealth, and glory seem to "drive nations to imagine a vain thing." (Quoting Isaiah) Can humanity ever rise up and refuse to take part in national or international vandalism, robbery, genocide, and general unease and abuse among the countries of the world! May Providence speed the day when they gave a war and nobody came!

Book Notes

1. Bergquist, Laura, "Thirty Days in Castro's Cuba," LOOK, Vol. 24, Nov. 8, 1960, p. 37.
2. Dubois, Jules, FIDEL CASTRO: REBEL LIBERATOR OR DICTATOR? New York: The New Bobbs-Merril Co., Inc., 1959, p. 146.
3. Brennan, Ray, CASTRO, CUBA, AND JUSTICE. Garden City, New York: Doubleday and Co., Inc., 1959, p. 41.
4. Ibid., p. 42.
5. Ibid., p. 48.
6. Ruark, Robert C. "Crowd-Madness Has Always Followed Crackpots," MIAMI HERALD, date and page unknown.
7. Brennan, Op. Cit., p. 47.
8. Ibid., p. 40.
9. Ibid., p. 48.
10. Ibid, p. 48.
11. St. George, Andrew, "A Revolution Gone Wrong," CORONET, July, 1960, p. 118.
12. Ibid., p. 117.
13. Ibid., p. 117.
14. Erikson, Erik H., YOUNG MAN LUTHER, New York; W. W. Norton and Co., Inc., 1958, p. 250
1958, p. 250.
15. Dubois, Op. Cit., p. 345.
16. Ibid., p. 52.
17. Ibid., p. 60.
18. Brennan, Op. Cit., p. 47.
19. Dubois, Op. Cit., p. 82.
20. Erikson, Op. Cit., p. 123.
21. Ibid., p. 143.

22. Dubois, Op. Cit., p. 371.
23. Ibid., p. 30.
24. Russell, Bertrand, POWER: A NEW SOCIAL ANALYSIS. New York: W. W. Norton and Co., Inc., 1938, p. 19.
25. Ibid., p. 17.
26. St. George, Op. Cit., p. 119.
27. Dubois, Op. Cit., p. 368.
28. Ibid., 367-8.
29. Ibid., p. 366.
30. Ibid., p. 128.
31. Russell, Op. Cit., p. 17.
32. Dubois, Op. Cit., p. 374.
33. Erikson, Op. Cit., p. 103.
34. Dubois, Op. Cit., p. 81.
35. Ibid., p. 332.
36. Ibid., p. 354.
37. Ibid., p. 67.
38. Ibid., p. 68.
39. Erikson, Op. Cit., p. 22.
40. Ibid., p. 42.
41. Ibid., p. 46.
42. Ibid., p. 67.
43. Ibid., p. 101.
44. Ibid., p. 103.
45. St. George, Op. Cit., p. 117.
46. Erikson, Op. Cit., p. 222.
47. Ibid., p. 110.
48. St. George, Op. Cit., p. 117.
49. Erikson, Op Cit., p. 142.
50. Ibid., p. 252.

51. Ibid., p. 242.
52. Ibid., p. 249.

Bibliography

Brennan, Ray, CASTRO, CUBA, AND JUSTICE. Garden City, New York: Doubleday and Co., Inc., 1959.

Dubois, Jules, FIDEL CASTRO: REBEL LIBERATOR OR DICTATOR? New York: The New Bobs-Merril Co., Inc., 1959.

Erikson, Erik H., YOUNG MAN LUTHER. New York; W.W. Norton and Co., Inc., 1958.

Ruark, Robert C., "Crowd-Madness Has Always Followed Crackpots," MIAMI HERALD, date and page unknown.

Russell, Bertrand, POWER: A NEW SOCIAL ANALYSIS. New York: W.W. Norton and Co., 1938.

St. George, Andrew, "A Revolution Gone Wrong," CORONET, July, 1960.

APPENDIX:

EXCERPTS FROM LETTERS WRITTEN HOME

February 8, 1959: …Wednesday is the anniversary of José Martí's birthday. We'll have a holiday on it, of course. At the church they are having a program in honor of the occasion, and I'm to work up some music to the words of some of Martí's poetry. Have just gotten the music to one poem and am hot on the trail of another piece. His work is very famous, and children must learn these poems by heart when they are in grade school.

… Guess I told you that we are getting all the old mail that has lain in the post office for months waiting to be censored. Just got a missive from LIFE Magazine telling me that Anna and Bill are giving me a subscription. It was sent on Dec. 9th! (Two months to get here—just ninety miles across the Straights of Florida.) Last week I got a birthday greeting from the Carroll English Guild which they sent in October. (Four months to arrive!)

...Am looking forward to receiving Dan's tape. I don't know if it would cost duty or not. Try sending it and we'll see. I imagine it will cost something—possibly not very much. This new government is making a lot to-do about its honesty. Let's test it!

February 14, 1959: ...We had planned to visit President Batista's former country home this morning but the passes were not available. The alternative was skin diving, but it looks like that didn't pan out either, so here we sit, doing the things we should be doing—planned things. It is more leisurely this way—but not so interesting.

...The radio is blaring one of the many patriotic songs which have come out since the first of the year. They are everything from popular songs to marching songs with blare of trumpets, etc. Now the newspaper says Fidel is Prime Minister—and all the cabinet has resigned. What are we in for?! Miss Grubb had given him three months before he is fully in power, but she has to acknowledge that he is moving even faster than she figured. The worship of Fidel is widespread and seems nothing short of sinister. Busses and cars have banners pasted in their windows with "Gracias, Fidel!" and no one would dare say a word against him. The newsreels never leave him out, and the movie audience always cheers and claps and stomps when one comes on.

February 21, 1959: … Thursday is Teacher's Day and the school is giving a supper for the teachers. There is strong nationalistic feeling in these times and so, instead of a banquet of fancy (American) food, we are having the typical Cuban feast—roasted pig, black beans and rice, fried plantains, yucca, and lettuce-and-tomato salad. It is delicious—though we will all suffer liver trouble the next day!

February 26, 1959: …We are doing everything very Cuban these days, the air being charged with nationalistic fervor.

… Tomorrow is our first kickball game of the season. The daughter of Sosa Blanco, one of the most notorious political criminals who was recently executed, is on the team, and she has just come back to school after having been out all during the trial and his execution. The family is left without any funds except Sosa Blanco's December salary check. Our school is letting the girls attend free and eat lunch in the dining hall without charge. The girls are as sweet as can be and seem to have suffered much on account of this whole business of their father, naturally. Other children say things to them without realizing the pain it causes them. But they are making a valiant effort and are almost their former selves. You probably read about their father in your papers, eh?

Another girl of the team is the daughter of "Ventura's" sister. Ventura was the very bloody police chief here in Habana. He escaped the country alive when Batista fled—but many Cubans are hoping that some Cuban wherever he is will put an end to him. This has had a very visible effect on the girl. She is becoming more and more introverted and self-conscious. I so feel for her! She and I have had several talks about the things that matter in life (so as not to become fixated on the painful things)—but am afraid that it will be very difficult to reach her to make a difference for her. Her family seems to have few standards or moral values or religion, etc. Not that they are amoral necessisarily, but they just live life—seemingly with little aim, nothing of outstanding importance to them in their time of loss except for the physical, monetary, and emotional losses which are so present to them.

There are several American (U.S.) girls on the team. They are all quite young. This team is such a conglomeration of ages!—but that's what makes life interesting in this place. I hope these young ones feel team spirit and don't flounder under the losing, which is sure to happen. We have been practicing with some Candler boys (boys' school across the street from our school) to toughen us up some. Here goes!

———————————

... It turns out that I don't have to pay Cuban income taxes after all. Whew! I receive less than $100 a month here, out of which I pay board, etc. The rest I have deposited in my bank in the States, which counts me out on taxes. Now we have to see about American income tax in the future. There will be a consultant at the American Embassy here for a few days more. We hope to get to see him before he leaves.

———————————

...Tuesday was the 24th, the day on which Cuba's revolution with Spain began back in the 1800's. There was an air show in the morning, no school all day, and a big parade that night to commemorate the occasion. We went to the parade, standing amid the press of humanity and the exploding firecrackers for hours. There were motorcycle police from Dade County and Miami, Florida, several high-school bands from Miami, the University of Miami band, a band from Venezuela, marching boys from Venezuela, floats from all over Cuba, bands of marching boys from most of the biggest boys' military schools here. It was sumptuous!

Then for us to get together and come back in the car afterwards (we left the parade before it was over) took us an hour. The parade was to begin at 6:00, and we got home around 11:00.

Miss Buck and her sister sat in the Presidential Reviewing Stand. That's where the T.V. cameras were. It would have been a lot easier to have gone to somebody's house down the street to have watched it all on T.V. (The school has no television.) But of course you don't get the real flavor of the thing when you do that.

...Am making visible progress at reading through newspapers (looking for clippings showing the political direction the country was taking). You should see the stack of clippings I have stashed away! My goal is to get them into scrapbooks someday. I hope for such a time this summer. Will I get it?

On our excursion to Soroa, three teachers sit together for a picture: Miss Gilbert, Buenavista teacher; Marshall Lindsay, Candler College teacher; Author Carroll English, Buenavista teacher.

April 11, 1959:

...We took a small group of commerce students (25) on an excursion to Soroa, a little place nestled in the green mountains of Pinar del Rio, the only province west of Habana Province. Soroa's main feature is its lovely falls, with a thatched-roof place to eat beside the stream, a lookout spot from atop the same mountain, horse rides for some, etc. For ten cents I got a huge cherimoya from a man selling fruit which fellow teacher Miss Gilbert and I divided and ate with gusto. So juicy and sweet! This was the most enjoyable trip I've been on! We took scads of pictures and could have taken many more. If we had not been with a group on a bus we would have stopped along the way to take shots of other beautiful sights. Am still seeing many many things I'd like to take pictures of before leaving Cuba.

...This week I translated a pamphlet for a Cuban pastor who says he will edit it and have it printed. I have another one which I would like to do for a local-preacher friend in Oriente Province who wrote me, asking for some tracts or other kinds of literature that the people where he is working could read. It is a very remote, difficult place to work in at the far-eastern end of the island, some parts of which are not even accessible by road. Since he hasn't had luck with these folks getting his message or coming to church, he hopes that if he could put some attractive literature in their hands, the people might take interest.

I feel sorry for some of those local ministers. They are usually boys who want to be ministers but can't afford schooling. The church assigns them to some little chapel way out in the sticks, telling them to study up so that they can pass the government exams and take seminary. They plug away at this until they are growing older, getting lines in their face, their enthusiasm becoming dampened, and they're not the fresh, idea-filled youths they once were. There seems little to be done about this, though. There is scant money set aside for scholarships for these boys-becoming-men. Practically all those who finish at the seminary in Matanzas have been on at least part scholarship throughout their entire training, but there just aren't enough of these "becas" to go around.

Student Cándido Pérez, mixing animal feed at the agricultural school in Oriente. He worked as a local minister in the bush until he migrated to Miami in the '60s, where he served as minister for Spanish-speaking congregations for decades.

The boy referred to above is Cándido Pérez, a graduate of the Ag School and such a fine young man. But he would have to cover four years of bachillerato (secondary education), four years or more of university (in agriculture, he hopes), and maybe a year at seminary in order to reach his goal. Given the resources available, I'm afraid he may be one of those who just falls by the wayside, being a local preacher for life, forever living at subsistence level. Not that that is bad. The world needs plenty of good, stout-hearted, simply good men. But this is one who got a good start at the Ag School, caught a vision with hope and purpose—the kind the church needs, men and women who are interested in helping others to help themselves. And Cuba so needs able people in agriculture. Most of those who reach professional levels in any field, however, tend to all stay in Habana. Good people are needed out in the hinterlands.

... Got ambitious last night and put in chronological order all the stuff I have collected on the revolution. I kept the newspaper every day for the first month after the revolution triumphed. Also the first three issues of BOHEMIA (the principal magazine in Cuba at the time), and all the hand bills and leaflets I could get my hands on since the first of January. These latter have been multitudinous! Probably no one will ever read them but me. They are too bulky to send to interested persons and too heavy to carry around with me—certainly on the plane. I am going to give away and throw away everything possible.

... The other night I was awakened by shots and a ruckus in the street below. There was some shouting and running steps chasing up the street after whoever it was. Groggily, I pulled over to the far side of the bed away from the wall and window, half-way remembering about Mrs. Needham going to the back of her apartment and sleeping on the floor when there were so many shootings in her neighborhood after the beginning of the year (when dictator Batista fled and Castro forces came to power). Hardly anyone else in the boarding department had heard last night's upset, but this morning the window on the stairs (right next to my room) had a round hole in it where a shot went through.

View from my bedroom window at Colegio Buenavista in the Habana suburb of Marianao. Gulf of Mexico seen in the distance.

April 19, 1959: Dear folks, you should see Barbara's and my rooms! We are going through the very soul-refreshing experience (as Barbara says) of preparing to pack. I didn't know I had collected so much stuff—pictures especially! For five years I've been taking pictures and just adding them to the stack. Now I've been sorting them, getting rid of some, winnowing out some which other people may want, and cropping the ones I want to keep to put into an album which I propose to buy. It will have to have many pages! It is great fun, and it does you so much good to think through which things are essential and which aren't. It would be better if I weren't so interested in history. I save so many clippings which seem of historical interest, as well as the notebooks I have kept at a number of conferences and classes—and my letters. The letters are the things which will really try my thrift! Also books! Haven't gotten around to their second weeding-out yet. Gave a number of them to Mrs. Needham for the Chandler School library a while back.

Here is a letter I wrote to my family a few days after the revolution came into its own, which summarizes most of the earliest happenings. It duplicates some of the material mentioned in the text.

January 10, 1959:

Dear kith and kin,

There is still so much to say! I don't know which to sift out to tell and which to just let fall by the wayside. Life seems intensely historical and exciting at this moment, and I am glad to be living in these times in this place.

I am being made to think very hard about the relative virtues of war and pacifism. The U.S. is probably the only country able to straighten herself out and develop a new government after having attained independence by war. That was likely because she did not have a population so accustomed to the backlog of old ways of doing things. Vice, string-pulling, advantage-seeking, vengeance, low morality, and such are the commonest traits among the Spanish-speaking cultures who learned them from the conquering Spaniards. These qualities cannot be overcome overnight, no matter how sincere the leaders' ideals may be.

Castro has convinced us all of his integrity and sincerity of purpose. But already you can see the old ways of doing and thinking coming back to life—of course. Pardon and forgetting vengeance are what many people are saying would surely save us from further blood bath. But those still don't save the country from ignorance and the old patterns so widely dispersed. The new government seems firm in wanting to wipe out gambling—and alcoholic beverages were banned for the first few days in order to keep down chaos. It seems like it would work better for Cuba if foreign industries were nationalized and American profiteers squeezed out, since they do nothing for the masses of people they control as workers, and only those in high political office gain so handsomely financially from their association with the kings of commerce.

Talking with the *barbudos* (the "bearded ones"—revolutionary fighters), one is charmed by their anxiousness to stop the fighting and get back to homes, families, and jobs. One becomes sure that they fought for ideals. Surely the glory and excitement in fighting and winning are real compensation for the fact that they received no pay. They were supported in spirit by the common people, their food was bought from country folk with moneys collected in the various towns and cities and villages. (Many were imprisoned for giving the rebels food—including the Methodist minister I told you about.) Their uniforms came from local stores along the way; their insignia (if they had any) and religious medals came from the people who were willing and anxious to do anything for the cause. What insignia they had were hand embroidered by rural girls.

As they came down the island from their mountain hideouts, they came in jeeps, tanks, trucks, and cars which had been donated or confiscated, and not a soul stayed at home or in the fields! Every Cuban found a place along the route that the liberators were to take to reach the capital city. This was really a people's revolution. Surely there was not one, except those on Batista's payrolls, who did not feel that he had had a personal part in this victory—because he had, in one way or another, even if it might have only been interest in the revolution's progress and passing on rumors, etc.

Jubilant, exultant crowds waited all along the roads in the wind and sun, waiting to see the victors, shake their hands, and so to see Castro. He is now an idol of a caliber that all the movie stars and others sorts of the wealthy and famous could never reach in the minds of young and old, rich and poor, educated and ignorant, urban and rural in Cuba in these days. We are living in a fantasy difficult to imagine. If anything were to happen to Fidel, the place would be torn apart. This, despite the fact that he declares that "the new democracy is already set in motion and that nothing would happen to freedom here if something should happen to (him)."

When he finally got to Habana, the whole nation had come to the city to be in on his triumphant entry. All work was shut down. There would have been no one to buy anything except along the parade route so that every soul could greet the liberator. Fully half or three quarters of the crowd were dressed in red and black with a Cuban flag clutched in hand.

The procession inched along the way because the press of the crowd was so great. It took roughly nine hours for him to parade through the whole city. His nine-year-old son (one of our Candler students) was beside him on the top of the tank he rode. When he passed in front of the radio center/T.V. station about four o'clock, the child was still standing up, waving a flag, but by the time he got to where we were (in the same section of the city), it was dark, and the child was sitting down.

After Castro's tank came a lot of army—and then the people. Every truck from the electric company, telephone company, beer companies, express-delivery companies, busses, private cars—virtually the entire population—followed him out to Colombia Base were he was to stay. (It was important and symbolic that he did not stay at the Presidential Palace, but continued to the military quarters.) American newsmen were amazed. They had seen nothing like it. Surely nothing like it has been seen in the Americas! There must have been over a million people in the procession—or surely more. The American press has likened it to Hannibal crossing the Alps, but it is truthfully like nothing else! It was purely Cuban—spontaneous, boisterous, affectionate.

We went to the Commodore Club yesterday to get some skin-diving equipment and got stuck there by the rain, so took advantage of the time to converse with some of the (hundreds) of rebel troops billeted there. There was an elderly man with curly white beard and mane who spoke with the polite gentleness and exactness of the perfect country gentleman descended from Spaniards (or from Spain itself). There were burly, grizzly brick masons, farmers, etc. There were varying shades of colored men from mulattoes to those who could have stepped out of the Bantu jungles. One was formerly in the Batista army and knew all the rifle drill and formality of the trained soldier, while the quiet country boys only knew the simplest presentation of arms and guerrilla positions. They sheepishly apologized, "But we're not trained. We just fought to get this over. I would show you the guerrilla drill we did but I'd get my clothes all dirty, and these have to last us. It's all we've got." They could discuss rifles and guns like any soldier, though, having had to use all models and makes from a half dozen different countries. The heavy machinery had been captured from Batista's army.

There were tales, already legends, about the way some fought. Camillo Cienfuegos, the head of the army now, is said to have lain down with his men in the street to shoot with greater advantage at the government planes as they dove down to strafe a town. This is the way the Chinese fought, they tell, and got the best of the Japanese.

There are many stories of how Morgan, an American, veteran of World War II and the Korean War, had fought. He fought standing up, reputedly—never crouched—ready to run forward and press his advantage. When his rifle would jam, he would slam it against a tree, shouting insults at Batista all the while. He told the men in the rudimentary Spanish he learned living and working with them that he was a Cuban, loved Cuba, would stay in Cuba. All these things really encouraged the men and made for a great fondness in their hearts for him. He even married a Cuban girl from one of the villages. "And she's mighty pretty!" the speaker commented, to which all his companions nodded and said, "Yes, very pretty." There was another American among them, too, whose name I don't recall. Both had been guerrilla leaders. We were wondering what would happen to their citizenship now and found out that legally, it is no more! Morgan got into the fight because the Batista regime killed one of his buddies at Varadero.

And then there was Che Quevara, whom I think I described already. His millionaire parents are here as guests of the new government and are being interviewed on television. He is Argentine and a fabled character already in the annals of Cuban history. There are doubtless Mexicans and Venezuelans involved also, and maybe Costa Ricans. The triumph of the 26th-of-July Movement over one of the cruelest dictators of the Western hemisphere makes our success in Cuba an encouragement to people under dictatorships all over Latin America—if it will only work out! If it will only work out!

Tuesday, I went to Matanzas with Joyce Hill, a displaced missionary. When the situation where she was working became too unsafe to work in, she came over here to get further instructions and stay with us. She has remained a few days after D-day until things have quieted down a little and transportation has resumed. A seminary student returning to work, along with Marshall Lindsay, John Sanbach, and Joyce and I all piled into the jeep from Joyce's station in Santa Rosa. We stopped in Matanzas a few minutes to visit, and then went on to Varadero. We wanted Marshall to see it and had plans to swim, but it was too cold and windy. We waded along the shore and ate ice cream, then left. Marshall and Sandbach came on back to Habana on the bus as soon as we reached town, but I stayed and spent the night.

The next morning we took two missionaries our own age, more or less, to Santa Rosa to clean up the house there. We had just gotten started when the radio announced that Castro was coming through Jovellanos (the nearest town) in a little while. We left our brooms and dishwater just as they were, piled into the jeep, picked up friends along the way until the jeep was bulging, and bumped over the rough ruts through the cane fields. The whole town was at a high pitch of excitement all day long as the people waited for the rebel leader, not fainting a bit as the day wore on and he still hadn't shown up. Finally, around 6:30 the big steam whistle of a railroad shop there began to bellow—and kept it up full blast for maybe 20 minutes until the rebel army had ridden through the area. All the local folk hung onto the cars and ran behind them until the string of vehicles disappeared out of sight.

After cleaning the house a bit there, we jumped into the jeep to head back toward Matanzas, it being after dark now. When we were able to press our way out to the central highway, we discovered that we had to join the tail of the revolutionary convoy. In the cold and pitch-black dark, the country people were waiting at every crossroads and roadside house to holler, wave, and shout, "Fidel! Fidel!" The cheerers perceived our jeep in the gloom and imagined that we were part of the procession. They couldn't tell which car Fidel was in so cheered all the rebels and vehicles onward toward the capitol in case he might be in each one. There was nothing for us to do but join the procession. We blew the horn and hollered back at each little group whom we passed, to encourage their enthusiasm and the feeling of our all being happily in this together. We grew to feel that we were a part of the conquering army. That just shows what can happen if you pretend long enough.

It took us an hour or more to make the last few kilometers into Matanzas, and then we spent a long time trying to cross the city, the traffic being so clogged with people coming to see Fidel. At 11:00 he came on over the radio (long and short wave) covering North and South America, as well as television. Because every house on the street was watching Castro speak on TV or hearing him on the radio, we could hear his every word out in the street from the porch of Irene Toland School where we were spending the night.

But I was so dog-tired from driving practically all day and from standing in the waiting crowd for the rest of the day that I fell into bed asleep after our 10:00 supper. The papers have carried all Fidel has said, and the entire population can tell you anything he has spoken of.

He has wonderful ideas—trial for all political prisoners, nationalization of industries, freedom of speech and press, etc. And he reprimands his own who cause factions and friction. Unfortunately, Fidel is not the only one concerned with carrying out these matters. As I said before, these ideals have sifted down to the rank and file of the men who have fought with him. At present, the ones who seem to be ready to cause trouble are the college students—wanting to begin a students' political party and do its managing, etc., etc. (They are probably stepping out to show publicly that they are ready to support the rebel program—given that they stayed in Habana throughout the fighting down-island.) Castro already began some agrarian reform in Oriente Province when he was down there.

We have been taking pictures right and left. Everything is all so colorful. The bushy-haired and bearded men in their olive-drab uniforms, with all sorts of flags and medals, insignia and paraphernalia, and guns and boots, riding around in fancy cars, and cheering crowds and roaring tanks and blowing horns, etc., etc. Too bad you can't take sound with the pictures you snap!

Yes, mail is reaching me now—and uncensored. It is so great. We still all pinch ourselves now and then to see if it's true that we are living in freedom. We just travel around sometimes to prove that it can be done without being afraid of getting shot or blown up on a bridge or getting stopped while they burn a bus. I have devoured every newspaper that has come out, believing that we are getting the "straight." There was a joke in ZIG-ZAG, the political joke sheet, in which a man runs around shouting, "Down with Fidel! Down with Fidel!" His wife looks at him, horrified, and says, "Man, what are you doing?! You're not angry with Fidel!" He replies, "No, but I'm just seeing how it feels to be able to say what you please!"

January 17, 1959:

It seems impossible that another week has rolled around already! We began school Monday, having gotten an extra week off while waiting for the conquering heroes to arrive. Now that the commonplace job of putting all the noble ideas into practice is upon us and the rebels are drunk with glory—now comes the disenchantment. Castro has appeared too much for too long in public over too long a period without sleep. It has to tell on him when he doesn't get any sleep over such a long period of time. He often doesn't know what he's saying, I think. A lot of the official meetings of the various ministries and bodies in the government meet at all hours of the wee-small ones—1:00 or 2:30 or 5:00. There's really no valid rationale for that!

The Rebel Leader made an official surprise visit to the British ambassador the other night at 1:00 A.M. to discuss the resented British sale of arms and tanks to Batista in the last days of the revolution's struggle. Ever since then, Cuban-British relations have been improving—while the U.S.-Cuban relations have been spiraling downward, because of the two men in the United States' Congress, Senator Morse and Representative Hayes, who have been questioning the justice of the military trials and killings which are taking place here. Castro sees this as the U.S. trying to force his hand. This makes him very adamant and paranoid, and he declares that if the Marines land in Cuba, "We will make trenches in the streets and fight to the last man (2 million)." All this drama seems like overkill. There did happen to be some Navy ships on maneuvers in the Caribbean, evidently, but when they heard of the furor being stirred up, they didn't make their intended stop in Habana Harbor, going on to Trinidad, instead, I believe.

But Castro should be more careful. The whole rebel movement must be more careful in their output to the public. Their words and actions quickly roil up the whole country. The university students of Habana are now ranting that all high-school and university work for the last two years shouldn't count toward graduation, since during this time some of the students were absent, being off in the hills fighting. They were lobbying to abolish all private universities, but there was such protest that it didn't come about, fortunately. Our Candler University would have been swept away, too, if they had had their way. Those who have tried to enforce such a decision have wanted to make all students start back where they were at the beginning of the revolution. The government didn't make these dicta—rather, the students, but since they cooperated in the movement, they feel that the government "owes" them this favor, they say. Or maybe the government fears that they will put up too-big a stink about it, so make motions to capitulate to student demands.

This is the way revolution is. You are never completely free, because you owe too much to those who cooperated with your program to put you in power. That is why Batista could not only not establish even a semblance of decent government under his regime, but could not even get out of the hot seat when he wanted to and leave the country—because too many persons were too in love with the graft he was doling out to them for boosting him to the top and maintaining him there.

The first few days were wonderful because you could talk and think as you pleased. But now we are beginning to fear if you were to dare to say anything against the heroes—and being American would make it worse in these days. You would be a high treasonist by public opinion, though I doubt that the government would do anything very bad to us unless they could prove you to be a *Batistiana.*

Of course many *Batistianos*, militarists, etc., are now on the band wagon headed for the morgue. It's just when you have killed citizens, the rebels say, when you must fear. Many of the private citizens—and even the American youth here are rabid on this execution business. They are saying that if you have killed even one person, you should be tortured and then killed. As things are at this moment, it is being said that if you have killed five, you surely are worthy of death. The trials, however, are now carried out by third parties, rather than by rebel commanders. And in the extremely emotional climate which prevails now so soon after the fighting, I feel, too, that these executions should be delayed to insure greater justice.

Barbara (fellow missionary) says she gives this government five years before it gets toppled by another rebellion. I don't feel that I can speculate properly on this. Life is so full of the unexpected, I feel like I am beginning to learn the folly of predictions. This government seems to be either on the brink of becoming a hollow puppet government—or of struggling its way toward the dawning day of democracy. Either seems entirely possible and feasible at this moment. Surely only the Deity would know which we are headed for. If this government continues on the way it's headed, though, I don't even give it five years.

I can say all this because there is no censorship at this point. If they decide to implement censorship, they at least haven't done so yet. They are still organizing. There are only a few policemen being returned to their previous status and their uniforms. It is being discussed whether the police uniform should be changed from the previous blue one to the black pants and sky-blue shirts of the Miami police.

I think people—or at least the traveled, sophisticated ones—are seeing through Castro's denunciation of the United States—though I could also easily see us Americans being booted from the island. Nationalizing all foreign industries would be a quick and easy way to do this. But there are too many Cubans who like the States and have visited there and have friends and family there, to let this happen. Many have been in exile there. But in this highly charged atmosphere it would be possible for Castro and his minions to sway all public opinion overnight. The whole nation has been hanging on his every word. The rebels are still very popular and involved. There is even a little bearded doll being sold in the streets, dressed in an olive drab uniform, with a white "26" on a tiny red-and-black armband sewn around its little arm.

A while ago, a Salvation Army man came to get the food and clothes which we had collected for them to distribute among the refugees and displaced persons in the interior of the country. Barbara and I had found out about the drive when we responded to an invitation to an organizational meeting being held last Sunday in the little red-seated auditorium of the Coca-Cola plant for their members, various church directors, and any and all denominations. We were the only conventional church denomination present in those attending. The others who came were those of the Army, the American Bible Society (though the head who was present, is a Presbyterian), and some small sects.

A semi-truck full of food and clothes had already been taken to Santa Clara, halfway down the island. It turned out that this load was inadequate for the 5,000 people who accrued to receive the goods. The driver and helpers brought back tales of how under-supplied the needy crowd was—some sleeping on bare bed springs with only a croker sack to cover themselves with, if they were lucky. People's bones were protruding from their skin and their eyes looked glassy and unhealthy from hunger. Farther on down the island it is surely worse, because they have been in open conflict for a much longer period. Our students here were pretty good about bringing clothes to share—but not as generous as a school of this size and station should be, it seemed to us. Our school will give some money to the drive. Several of the largest department stores of the city are contributing.

Anyway, the Salvation Army man came to pick up the things this afternoon, hoping to get a taxi to take him and the bundles to the Army headquarters way over across town in Old Habana. We took him in our car and were glad for the chance to become better acquainted with him, and to see one of the eight chapels they have erected for their work, scattered about the city.

In these two meetings we've gotten to know a delightful young couple from Chile. His father was Norwegian and his mother, Spanish. His mother died early and he lived with his Spanish grandparents in Spain until his father later married a Canadian woman. They were missionaries in Uruguay where his sister was born. Her mother was Swedish and father, Norwegian, I think. They were both educated in England, met in Chile, and work here in Cuba. All members of both sides of their families were in the Salvation Army. They speak English beautifully and are really charming. They were the kind of international travelers whom no one could resent—and who make valuable contributions in a foreign country. Of course, there would be few foreign countries that would even be foreign to persons such as they!

Our bishop died yesterday or the day before in Florida. Miss Buck (our director) and missionary Carl Schafer went to the funeral. I think my minister, Carrazana, went, too. Meanwhile, Barbara is pinch-hitting as director of Colegio Buenavista. We turned out of school a half day when we found out about the bishop's death. His passing was a great loss for the Protestant Church in Cuba. Cubans loved him greatly, as did we. He wrote us every now and then in the last year or so, letting us know that he was praying for Cuba and the workers and laymen in the Christian community here. We are mindful of our loss of his spirit from our scene. May we get another bishop almost as great! He had his faults, of course. The one that comes quickest to mind for us is how he made the appointments of personnel—sending the rural workers to the city and vice versa, etc. But he certainly had an abundance of good qualities. It is said that the church in Cuba had been treated as a step-child until he came along—at which time she became the favorite child.

We went to pick up Miss Buck at the airport a while ago as she returned from the funeral. Because of poor visibility, but mostly because there were cars on the runway trying to grab the first place in line where the plane would dock in an effort to spirit out of the country someone formerly in Batista's government, the plane couldn't land for 40 minutes. The airport was bristling with rebel soldiers, and we were also inspected by having beamed on us a large glaring reflector before we could enter the place. Some shots were exchanged, but then, that is nothing unusual. We hear them every few nights in our neighborhood. Too many people were too mixed up with the former dictator, who scatted—leaving them "high and dry." Now, not a one can leave until he has gone through his trial. However, embassies are permitted to let fleeing persons stay on their property, but they are not allowed to give them *salvo conducto* out of the country.

Well, must be off to Sunday School. Write!

Love to all, Bits (My family nickname)

Carroll English
carroll@stelle.net

www.ingramcontent.com/pod-product-compliance
Ingram Content Group UK Ltd.
Pitfield, Milton Keynes, MK11 3LW, UK
UKHW041944190726
13854UKWH00004B/1779